FOLLO

JESUS

Attaining the
High Purposes
of Discipleship

ROSS TOOLEY

YWAM
PUBLISHING
P.O.BOX 55787 SEATTLE, WA 98155

YWAM Publishing is the publishing ministry of Youth With A Mission. Youth With A Mission (YWAM) is an international missionary organization of Christians from many denominations dedicated to presenting Jesus Christ to this generation. To this end, YWAM has focused its efforts in three main areas: 1) Training and equipping believers for their part in fulfilling the Great Commission (Matthew 28:19). 2) Personal evangelism. 3) Mercy ministry (medical and relief work).

For a free catalog of books and materials write or call:
YWAM Publishing
P.O. Box 55787, Seattle, WA 98155
(425) 771-1153 or (800) 922-2143
www.ywampublishing.com

First Printing 2000

Following Jesus: Attaining the High Purposes of Discipleship

Published by YWAM Publishing
P.O. Box 55787, Seattle, WA 98155

ISBN 1-57658-205-1

Printed in the United States of America.

❦ acknowledgments

My warm thanks go to Sandi Tompkins, Matt Rawlins, Yolanda Olson, Roxanne Olson, Doug and Margaret Feaver, Marge Clewett, and Audra Jo Baumgarth—all members of the writers' group at the U of N campus in Kona, Hawaii. Their help, suggestions, support, prayers, and fellowship over a three-year period were invaluable. They sure kept me motivated to write!

Sincere thanks to my friends Scott and Sandi Tompkins for their valuable suggestions for improvements. I deeply appreciate the hours they lovingly and diligently labored using their gifted editorial skills to help complete the project.

My special thanks go to my wife, Margaret, for walking with me on many of these adventures and for allowing me the time to work on this task. Her input into my life over the past thirty years has been incalculable as she has loved, inspired, informed, and challenged me.

To our Filipino friends from the student center days in the Philippines during the 1970s—especially Rosemary Alvarez, Rolly Bagallon, Barbara Calo, Mel and Helma Calcaben, Evelyn Noble Cawaling, Juan and Helen Coromina, Virgie Chumalan, Emma Dagwa, Vangie Benbenen Fuentes, Alex Ibalio, Angie Buccahan Parsons, Fred and Vangie Sanchez, Sammy and Debbie Tenizo—I extend warm thanks for taking me into their hearts, for walking alongside me, and for helping to shape my life for God's glory. Without them this book would never have been written!

I am deeply grateful to the following who helped mold my life as mentors during my younger and formative years: Trevor Chandler, Joy Dawson, Loren Cunningham, Frank Houston, Campbell McAlpine, Floyd McClung, Dal and Dorothy Walker, Arthur Wallis, and Neville Winger, among many others.

My profoundest thanks, of course, go to our Lord Jesus Christ, who has lovingly taught me to be His disciple. His patience and understanding have been incredible.

To the only wise God be glory and praise forever!

✺ contents

PREFACE 6

1 Recognizing Our Giftings 7

2 Using Our Past Difficulties 15

3 Committing Our Lives to Christ 21

4 Learning to Speak God's Truth 27

5 Getting the Training We Need 37

6 Hearing the Voice of God 47

7 The Testings of God 61

8 Fulfilling Our Ministry 77

9 Finding Our Life's Partner 91

10 Walking by Faith 111

11 Moving in Strategic Evangelism 123

12 Being Faithful in Little Things 135

13 Learning the Power of Intercession 143

14 Receiving Revelation 155

15 Giving Up Rights 165

16 Valuing Praise and Worship 175

17 Continuing On in Discipleship 183

MINISTRY UPDATE 190

◖ *preface*

How do I hear from God? Why does God allow difficulties and trials? How do I find God's calling on my life? What's important in a marriage partner? How do I share my faith with others? These are just some of the questions I'm asked as I teach on discipleship around the world. *Following Jesus* attempts to answer those deeply felt questions. Following the format of my earlier book *Adventures in Naked Faith,* each chapter of this book relates more adventures—some of them risky—undertaken for Christ's cause. The teaching sections that follow discuss the important aspects of discipleship implicit in the above questions, including being guided by God, the importance of prayer and worship, and the need to brave the fires of testing.

The road of discipleship has pitfalls and dangers, and sometimes we may take a wrong turn along the way. But we know for certain that Christ's worthy and just cause will ultimately triumph. If I had my life to live over, even my life as a Christian, I would do many things differently. If only I could revisit the scenes of my greatest mistakes and do it right! But that's why it's so important to recognize that being a disciple means being a learner. In Jesus' school, we learn from our failures. It can be breathtaking to see how God redeems our pasts and shows us how to use our backgrounds and talents for His purposes.

May God patiently persevere with us and increase our understanding of discipleship as we strive to live the life of the Cross in a pleasure-seeking world.

one

Recognizing Our Giftings

We all have talents that may be spotted at a young age: God-given abilities that point to our one day being engineers, truck drivers, artists, homemakers, or preachers. Recognizing our giftings at an early age may help to point us to God's will for our lives later on. I have always been a bit of a daredevil and enjoyed difficult tasks. While not a world-class leader, I have loved to train others to do things I think are important. Looking back on my life, I have discovered that these talents didn't wait until my conversion to surface. The problem was, I used my giftings for selfish purposes before I began using them for the kingdom of God. But then, even our preconversion talents may well serve as signposts for the future.

I stared into the stern face of the woman who tapped me on the shoulder.

"Excuse me," the woman said curtly as I stood on the sidewalk outside a variety store. "The manager wants to see you!"

I could feel her x-ray vision examining the stolen articles concealed in my clothing. With a look of disapproval, she nodded toward the door I had just exited in triumph.

My twelve-year-old legs felt like jelly as I walked in front of her through the crowd of busy shoppers. I was sure that everyone could see the stolen items stuffed into my pockets. Struggling with anxiety, I thought hard. As I passed the mountain of brightly wrapped peppermint chocolates and candies in cellophane bags, I unloaded a chocolate bar. *That will get rid of one piece of incriminating evidence,* I thought.

"Oh no you don't," the security woman barked. "The manager wants to see that too!"

Guiltily I put the candy bar back into my pocket and kept walking through the store where happy shoppers beamed and smiled at one another while I felt more and more intimidated. All too soon we stood outside a door marked "MANAGER."

The security woman rapped on the door, then thrust it open. I entered, my heart still pounding. A slim man wearing dark-rimmed glasses looked up at me coldly from behind a desk.

"I am getting tired of this," he snapped.

"So am I," the security agent replied cuttingly.

The manager jerked open his desk drawer and picked out a file.

"Empty your pockets!" he demanded.

I slowly pulled out all the incriminating evidence, including the chocolate bar. The excitement I'd had from shoplifting melted away. Over the past year I'd found it a challenge to hide a variety of merchandise inside my jacket: books, packets of candies, a cap gun, or a pair of brightly colored socks. It was equally challenging to casually walk out of the store and disappear into the crowd. I had been at this for over a year. Hitting several stores, I had managed to rip off quite a collection of items, including a dozen books by my favorite author. I eagerly read them and then sold them at the corner store for two-thirds the retail price. Young as I was, I had become very enterprising, using my gifts to extract the last drop of potential out of my actions. Cigarettes, even tobacco and cigarette papers, were also favorite items I stole. One night I even stuffed a couple of bulky coat hangers inside my jacket and managed to escape the store without anyone tapping me on the shoulder. But today was different. I'd been exposed.

One item I slowly took from my pocket under the watchful eye of the store manager was a small mirror. There was no practical reason for stealing the mirror. What my blond hair or boyish face looked like was of no special concern to me. It was the thrill of doing something daring or difficult.

One aspect of my gifting was my ability to come up with a different way of doing something and then to teach or *disciple* it to others, even if in those days it was for the wrong purpose. I'd developed a sneaky way of getting things inside my jacket without being detected and had taught a classmate how to do it. The security agent must have been intrigued by my technique. She began to explain my ingenuity to the manager, who heard her out before turning to me with a commanding voice, his pen poised.

"Name?"

"Ross Tooley."

"Address?"

"Sixty-seven Hansen Street, Newtown."

"What school do you attend?"

The woman answered ahead of me.

"Roseneath," she shot out. She must have seen that written on one of my schoolbooks. By her tone she evidently had concluded that I had lied when I gave my address in Newtown. I could see why. Our home in the south of Wellington was quite a distance from Roseneath. There were several schools in between. But I was telling the truth. Our family had come from a sheep-raising area of New Zealand 160 miles to the north. We had moved several times since we arrived in Wellington, and it was considered best if I stayed at Roseneath. After all, it was my eighth school in seven years.

After the interrogation came the verdict.

"We must see either your mother or father within twenty-four hours. Or we'll contact your headmaster. The next time we catch you stealing, we'll hand you over to the police."

The police! I slunk out of the store, believing that somehow everyone knew my crime. I was glad to lose myself among the sidewalk crowd.

I had bus fare to take the mile-and-a-half trip home but decided to walk. Slowly. I needed time to think. How on earth could I get out of this mess?

I passed near a merchant's yard where I had stolen valuable bottles. In light of what had just happened, all my bravado had evaporated. The drab area only added to my depression.

The faces of three people kept appearing before me: my mom, my dad, and the headmaster. All three were important authority figures in my life. How could I tell even one of them?

Recognizing Our Giftings

How do we recognize our giftings? And why do we need to know them?

Often our giftings are apparent before we come to Christ even if we use them wrongly. It is no surprise that since my conversion to Christ, God has led me to use the very giftings I once abused—the sense of daring, wanting to make the most of a situation, and the desire to teach. Of course, I no longer train anyone to steal. A lot of my time today is spent lecturing, writing, and leading by example. And with my penchant for adventure, over the years God has sent me on many varied assignments, some of which have been unusual, even risky, as you will see in subsequent chapters.

The giftings of the apostle Paul were evident before his conversion when he wreaked havoc on the early Church: his zeal and willingness to sacrifice for what he thought was right; his ability to articulate, argue, and persuade; and his preparedness to endure hardship. His rugged perseverance helped him triumph where others would have failed. Without the redemption and dedication of those giftings, the body of Christ would have been denied much of the New Testament.

Even when we are at a very young age, our gifts and abilities give us an inkling of what God might call us to do at a later time. I remember watching the activities of a five-year-old in our backyard after he'd seen a film about Noah. Once he'd climbed onto the water tank platform, he would pull pieces of lumber up from below just as he had seen Noah do in the movie. A few years later he made sketches of buildings using the most elementary "drafting" equipment. It is no surprise to me that today he is an engineer. What God eventually calls us into will clearly fit in with who we are. Recognizing what we are good at could very well help us map out our future.

But what if we can't recognize any talents that would indicate what our life's calling might be? Don't despair. The following suggestions might help.

First, ask trusted friends to point out what they think your strengths are. Others usually see us more objectively than we ever will see ourselves. Second, several personality and temperament tests* are available that may help shed light on your strengths. Added to what you already know, the results of these tests could prove extremely helpful. As you continue to walk with the Lord, further abilities—well buried at the moment—could emerge.

Keep in mind that as Christians, we are all created in Christ Jesus to do good works, which God prepared in advance for us to do (Eph. 2:10). We are all valuable to God, and He has given each of us a specific task. God's will for our lives, however, will always involve being part of the means by which people hear the gospel. Jesus said, "And this gospel of the kingdom will be preached in the whole world...and then the end will come" (Matt. 24:14). That command is still true for the body of Christ today.

Be aware that God is more interested in letting us know what He wants us to do with our lives than we are in knowing it. Often, His timetable may be different from ours, *but there is something we can all do now.* Right now we can prepare ourselves by following God more closely, by spending more time in His presence, by reading His Word, and by seeking to share Christ with others. That kind of preparation will be a good foundation for whatever God calls us to do.

---

* Such tests include the System for Identifying Your Motivational Abilities test, the Structure of the Intellect test, the Myers-Briggs Personality test, and the DISC test. Contact your local library, university, or bookstore for more details, or check the World Wide Web. No man-made test is perfect, but I've personally found each test useful.

One note of caution needs to be sounded. Once we have recognized our giftings, we must bring those talents to the Cross before God can use us effectively. We must die to our gifts and all that they represent—pride, for example—before they can be redeemed for God's kingdom. Sadly, many are still using their talents to plug the holes in their self-worth created by their painful backgrounds.

It is easy to show off our talents, even in the work of the Lord, but just because we are good at something doesn't automatically mean that it's always right to demonstrate it. Our motive must be to glorify God. Those who have forgotten that principle often end up as spiritual shipwrecks. It is when we have died to the selfish pursuit of our God-given talents that God fully gets the glory.

two

Using Our Past Difficulties

Crippling poverty marks the early years of some kids, while other children enjoy unmerited abundance. Some youths enjoy stable families, while others have very difficult home lives. Whatever the nature of our background, it has helped to shape who we are.

How many of us have complained, "I would be doing this or that if only things had been different when I was a child." Or perhaps we've said, "If only I had different parents, or was raised in another environment, or had more money, or spoke a different language—I would be able to serve God much better!"

The truth is, no circumstance can undermine God's potential for our lives. God's choice of ministry for us will fit in with even the difficult events in our past. I didn't realize it at the time, but God would one day redeem my family circumstances for His glory.

My long journey home after the confrontation with the store manager provided the needed time to ponder the consequences of my actions. With my hands in my pockets, I scanned the cracks in the gutter. What could I do? As my pace slowed, my mind easily wandered to the unusual events of my childhood.

I grew up learning how to make do with what I had. Our family could not afford the uniforms that most students wore at my school. One cold morning I didn't even have a decent *ordinary* sweater to wear. Taking this concern to Mom, she immediately thought of a plan to keep me warm.

I had a thin, ragged sweater that could be worn under a new green shirt she had bought me. Outwardly I looked great, and I happily pedaled off to school on my bike, grateful for her ability to improvise. But I didn't foresee the disaster that lay just around the corner.

At school at that time of year we normally did physical education in our everyday clothes because of the chilly weather. At P.E. time that day, our bushy mustached, no-nonsense teacher from England looked out the window and made an unusual announcement: "I want all boys to strip to their undershirts!"

Stunned, I immediately felt ashamed. I wasn't wearing an undershirt! If I peeled off my nice green shirt and exposed my ragged sweater, I'd be subject to ridicule! While the other boys followed the teacher's instruction, I pretended to have a sudden interest in the wall by my desk. I hoped the teacher wouldn't notice me. But he did.

"Come on, Ross. Off with that shirt!" he commanded.

I was now the center of attention. Self-consciously I slowly unbuttoned my shirt. I could feel thirty pairs of classmates' eyes boring in on my shameful undergarment. Realizing what was happening, the teacher sensed my embarrassment and reversed his order.

"All right, you can leave your shirt on!"

But the damage had already been done.

To pour salt into the wound, my best buddy retold the incident after school to another friend who had missed "the show." I felt humiliated.

At times I felt very different from the others in my class. I had fewer privileges than most kids. For years our family had no car, no telephone, no refrigerator, no inside toilet, and no record player (these were the days before TV was introduced to New Zealand). Finding ways to stretch our limited resources was a constant challenge for my parents.

One time, because of my mother's health, my sister Elizabeth and I were placed in an orphanage, where every day we were awakened early to spend an hour working before school. With bucket in hand, I gathered trash from a segment of the large orphanage lawns and gardens. I had to pick up everything, down to the tiniest leaf. Every Saturday morning we worked four hours at a variety of boring tasks. How I hated that time of the week!

As I continued my slow journey home from being caught stealing at the variety store, I passed rows of inner-city houses, feeling as somber as the gray winter sky above me. A streetcar screeched to a halt, hissed, and then clanged. Passengers got on and off. I watched the car slowly pull away, gather speed, and move out of sight. Normally I would be on that car. But not today. I needed this time of walking home to figure out what to do!

A deep sense of shame engulfed me as I thought of my mother hearing that her son was a thief! I didn't want to break her heart. And what of my two younger sisters, Elizabeth and Julia? What kind of example was I setting for them? I could not justify my stealing. Mom and Dad had taught us all to be honest and had set us a good example. There was no way I could excuse my actions. I could say that being poor had driven me to it, but my conscience said otherwise. Now I had to face the consequences.

I thought about my father. He and I bonded over sports. I avidly followed the fortunes of the New Zealand national teams, and sometimes Dad and I watched a game at a stadium or listened to one on the radio. Dad had recently taught me to play chess, and I loved the challenge of clawing back lost territory when I was losing. But I couldn't tell Dad that I'd been caught stealing. There would be a scene, and I would be in deep trouble!

But if I didn't tell Mom or Dad, the manager would contact my headmaster at school. Mr. Robinson taught my class and had taken a liking to me. He had chosen me to hand over a check for the "Save the Children Fund" at a ceremony with the president of the Wellington branch who happened to be the wife of the British high commissioner. Because our school was the first to raise its target amount, the picture of Lady Mallaby and me had been published in the *Evening Post*. I was Mr. Robinson's favorite. I shuddered at the thought of him finding out what I had done!

I had now reached the house we rented on Hansen Street. Swinging back the old metal gate, I decided on a selfish course of action: I would tell Mom, break her heart, and play on the unhappy state of my parents' marriage by asking her not to tell Dad. That decision made, I went inside to talk to her before Dad got home.

Using Our Past Difficulties

It was not that God chose my unusual childhood circumstances, just as He does not plan rape or abortion. The knowledge of God's character clearly tells me that. Despite my background, when I yielded my life to Christ, He redeemed much of my past circumstances and turned them into something meaningful for Him.

Many times as a child I had to improvise, use personal belongings over and over, or just do without. What I learned through these circumstances served me well years later when I lived for thirteen years in the Philippines. I could easily identify with the needy, for I knew what it was to be considered poor and looked down on.

As much as I hated working those long hours as a trash and leaf gatherer at the orphanage, now I am thankful for that unpleasant task. It taught me to persevere when things got tough and not cave in during difficulties. That lesson has helped me enormously during my lifetime of work for the Lord. Even when it seemed that hell was conspiring against me, I simply refused to give up.

Years ago, Chuck Colson, the confidant of President Richard Nixon, obstructed justice during the infamous Watergate scandal and wound up in prison. He was converted to Christ in jail, and after his release he launched Prison Fellowship, a powerful ministry to prisoners that today serves eighty countries. His ministry has impacted the lives of countless thousands. In the United States alone, the families of two million prisoners have received Christmas presents, thanks to just one of Prison Fellowship's projects. God did not lead Colson into sin so that he could learn the horrors of imprisonment. But after Colson's conversion, God turned that negative into a positive.

As I grew up, I could have easily given in to bitterness about my family situation. Thankfully, I didn't. Maybe it was because I knew that my dad's upbringing was even more difficult than my own. After the early death of his father, his family had to borrow money to bury his father. With no government welfare in those days, the family of eight children toiled and went without to make ends meet. My dad became the major breadwinner at the tender age of twelve. He was twenty before he kept his first pay envelope. Perhaps it helped that I was taught that someone was always worse off than we were. Each of us would do well to remember other people's circumstances. Not many of us face the plight of famine that struck North Korea, where people have tried to satisfy their hunger pangs by eating bark torn from trees.

Learning to adapt was something else I gained through my childhood experience. Because of unusual circumstances, I lived for a few months with a family friend who rented a room from a blind man. I was not to let the owner know I was in the house. Consequently, I had to enter and leave the building surreptitiously through the bedroom window. My bed was an uncomfortable sofa, which served me well in the long term. As a missionary, I learned to sleep in a number of unusual situations, even on a flax mat or on bare boards.

It's important that we don't mourn our past. When we get to heaven, we may find that what we *overcame* on earth was just as important as what we *achieved*.

So let's ask God to redeem our past for His wonderful glory!

three

Committing Our Lives to Christ

My conversion was not a dramatic experience. I can't even pinpoint the exact day it happened. But that doesn't worry me, for what counts is being a new creation in Christ (Gal. 6:15). Looking back, I marvel at the grace of God that He could change me so much. As 2 Corinthians 5:17 says, "[I]f anyone is in Christ, he is a new creation; the old has gone, the new has come!"

Little wonder that Jesus called conversion being "born anew" (John 3:3 RSV). The experience gave me a brand-new start in life. It didn't just change my outward actions. It transformed me inwardly: my attitudes, my outlook, and especially my motivations.

When you are born again, you really do become different!

At age thirteen, I certainly had no use for religion. One day in class I'd openly mocked the
idea of life after death when I learned the ancient Egyptians
buried food with their dead so that their ancestors wouldn't go
hungry in the next life! To me, religion was for "old women and
fools" and for weird people who wanted to be good. My gods
were football and other sports.

When my mother invited me to hear the American evangelist Dr. Billy Graham preach in a Wellington football stadium, I
immediately recoiled in horror. What could be more boring! To
please her, however, I eventually agreed to go. Actually, to me,
the meeting was held on "revered" ground, because the park
was where I'd watched our New Zealand rugby football team
play international games. As I entered the stadium with my parents, I was amazed to see a large stage erected on a corner of the
playing field and a robed choir occupying the seats at one corner of the park. This was sure different!

After the preliminaries, the Reverend Dr. Graham opened
his Bible to the third chapter of the Gospel of St. John. Through
my infrequent attendance at Sunday school, I knew a Gospel
was a biblical account of the life of Christ. I'd once watched a
drunkard angrily fling a copy of the Gospel of John into the
gutter. I'd picked it up and even started to read it, but it had
made no impact on me.

The evangelist read the story of Jesus' encounter with the
Pharisee Nicodemus and quoted John 3:16: "For God so loved
the world that he gave his one and only Son, that whoever
believes in him shall not perish but have eternal life." I couldn't

remember reading or ever hearing that before. Dr. Graham spoke with such conviction and authority that I listened enthralled to the subject of Jesus telling Nicodemus that he had to be born again—something else I'd never heard of. This was the first sermon I'd ever enjoyed!

Though I had scoffed at the thought of an afterlife, I now found my beliefs changing completely. Further, for the first time, I saw that Jesus Christ was God's measuring stick. I suddenly *knew* my attitude toward Him would affect my destination after I died.

Despite that understanding with my head, my life didn't change. I was certainly not the new creation in Christ mentioned in 2 Corinthians 5:17. My profanity continued, and I still worshiped football more than God. And because I'd just started high school, a new god had emerged: my studies. I was certainly not born anew.

But I did pray. Sort of. I prayed for things like winning the table tennis championship at school. Although I'd started attending Sunday school, I skipped out before the church service began. I realize now that I participated in prayer and Bible reading much as someone would use a lucky charm—so that something bad wouldn't happen to me. I had no concept that salvation meant walking hand in hand with a loving, forgiving God (Luke 7:47; John 17:3).

At high school, a Christian meeting took place once a week that someone suggested I attend. During a meeting I saw slides shown by someone working for the Lord in Brazil.

"Now if any of you are thinking of becoming a missionary one day," the man declared, "listen carefully to what I am about to say…." What? Missionary! Who would ever want to be a *missionary*? Or talk to people about Christ, for that matter? I tuned the man out.

Two years went slowly by without a conversion experience or anything noteworthy happening to me spiritually. But then, just before I turned fifteen, I found my attitudes changing. I no longer wanted to live just for myself or my sports or for academic achievement. *For me this was revolutionary!*

I can't remember any specific incident—no particular meeting, trauma, or event that triggered the change. Perhaps it was the trickle-down effect of attendance at the weekly Sunday school class or the monthly Youth for Christ rallies. Quite probably the prayers and example of an older brother over a two-year period had some bearing on it. I had two brothers, Dale and Max, who no longer lived at home with us. My brother Max had come to the Lord just before the Billy Graham meeting, and I suspected he must have prayed many prayers for his swearing, sports-crazy younger brother. In any event, I trace my conversion to Christ to this time in my life when I wanted to live for the Lord and not for myself. The change in me over the next months was really amazing, and very soon after my conversion, I wanted to tell others about Christ!

Committing Our Lives to Christ

Jesus defined eternal life as knowing the true God (John 17:3). As helpful as the outward signs of "going forward" and "signing a decision card" may be, what matters is having a personal walk with the Lord. Or as the apostle Paul put it, "Neither circumcision [an outward Jewish sign] nor uncircumcision means anything; what counts is a new creation" (Gal. 6:15).

My conversion was not a dramatic Saul-on-the-road-to-Damascus experience but rather a drawn-out affair. Many others, I suspect, have had a similar experience. Seeds were definitely planted at the Billy Graham meeting that were harvested later. The evangelist certainly got me thinking and on the starting line for a spiritual journey. But it wasn't until I gave my life over to God that I could claim to have been converted or born anew.

The thing missing during those in-between years was *repentance,* an essential ingredient for conversion. Being caught stealing years earlier, for example, should have led me to godly sorrow, but it didn't. Sure, I spent hours worrying about the variety store manager talking to Mom. But my worry was entirely self-centered. I'd been caught and embarrassed. I had no concern that I had sinned against God or that I had offended others. When I learned the manager had dropped all charges, even that selfish "remorse" evaporated. Wanting in a sick way to receive the esteem of my schoolmates, I boasted about the incident. I did give up stealing, but again it was for a purely selfish reason: I didn't want to endure the shame of being caught again. But the time came when I did repent, and that made all the difference.

Repentance is something God commands of us all (Acts 17:30–31), and it is something we can all do. In the Greek New Testament, the word is *metanoia,* which means "a change of mind." That change must occur in two key areas. First, we need to change our thinking "toward God" (Acts 20:21 KJV), who desires a loving relationship with us. This means we stop ignoring God and start loving Him by following His plans for our lives. Second, since repentance also requires a change of mind regarding sin, we are to stop enjoying sin and start to hate it.

The born-again experience certainly changed things for me. My foul language stopped. Instead of laughing at drunkards, I now grieved for them. I was genuinely sorry for my acts of selfishness, including my past stealing history. Today, I find it difficult to take a paper clip without asking someone first. This is the wonder of being born again. It is not a set of rules imposed on us but a life-giving, internal experience God gives in response to our repentance.

My sorrow for my past was now genuine, different from my previous couldn't-care-less attitude. I had now experienced what the apostle Paul called godly sorrow, as opposed to the selfish sorrow I felt after visiting the variety store manager's office. Selfish sorrow brings about death, but godly sorrow produces life, which is salvation (2 Cor. 7:10).

Central to the born-again experience is that Christ died for our sins. Repentance is meaningless without faith in the work of Christ on the Cross and His triumphant Resurrection. Paul emphasized the need for a response of repentance to the death of Christ when he said, "I have declared to both Jews and Greeks that they must turn to God in repentance and have faith in our Lord Jesus" (Acts 20:21). In his early ministry, Billy Graham preached a message to which very few responded. During a long walk with the evangelist, a man of God told him that he hadn't preached the Cross. Dr. Graham vowed to always mention the Cross in his sermons after that. In my view, it is the preaching of the Cross that demonstrates the love of God and gives mankind the assurance that sin can be forgiven. However, the death of Christ does not automatically make the world right with God. A response of repentance is necessary as well. The death of Christ is God's initiative in salvation. Repentance is our part. Both aspects are essential to conversion.

Some may wonder how I, having mocked the concept of life after death, changed my view so dramatically when Billy Graham preached. I believe that when the gospel is faithfully preached, faith in God's nature is a result if the heart is open. Romans 10:17 says, "Consequently, faith [in God] comes from hearing the message."

Just as I was inspired by the witness of Billy Graham, I was soon to learn that witnessing to others would encourage faith to grow within them, too.

four

Learning to Speak God's Truth

I'd prayed the same prayer for months. "Lord, help me be a Christian influence in my class at school."

God wants us all to share our faith, and He will open doors as we pray (Col. 4:3–4). When God answered my prayer, I could never have known how far-reaching the implications of one attempt to witness would be. Through the events that followed, God ushered me into an entirely new phase and at the same time deepened my Christian experience.

It all started in a very normal setting, a regular, everyday history class one day at high school.

*T*he history lesson was about nineteenth-century England, and for some reason, religion had become the focus. Several of my classmates, including Raman, a New Zealand–born East Indian, participated in the discussion that followed. Just as the buzzer signaled the end of class, Raman forcefully protested about the role of religion in the world. As we tumbled out into the crowded corridor jostling with students, Raman and a few others continued the exchange of ideas. Suddenly I felt I should say something in defense of Christianity. This would be a completely new venture for me.

"You know, Raman," I began hesitantly, not knowing what I was getting myself into, "Christianity is different from religion. Real Christians—"

"Religion has caused more trouble in the world than anything else!" Raman retorted as he stopped to direct his animosity toward me. The dark lines drawn on his face told me how deeply he felt. By his anger you would not have thought he was from a devout Hindu family.

In the school yard, I tried to answer Raman's objections, but I was soon out of my depth. What did I know of telling others about Christ? Almost nothing. I could only remember one other time trying to do something similar. It was when I talked to an uncle while harvesting turnips on his farm. I'd made no impression that day. What hope would I have now with Raman?

As our little group headed to our homeroom building on the edge of the campus, I suddenly thought of my brother Max. He would know what to say. Why not ask Raman if he would talk to him? Didn't Max tell me Raman had come to his door selling vegetables? They must know each other, at least by sight. It was worth a try.

"How would you like to talk to my brother about this?" I offered. I waited quietly for his "Nah, I'm not interested," response, but it never came.

"All right," he said. "I'll talk to him."

I was taken by surprise but tried not to show it.

"Then how about Sunday? I could drop by your house and take you to Max's apartment."

"Okay."

Flushed with excitement, I contacted my brother, who was living with some young men from our church, not far from Raman's house. Sure enough, on Sunday, Raman was waiting for me. He introduced me to his family, and then I walked him to Max's place. One of Max's friends took him aside while I waited and prayed. When he and Raman emerged about an hour later, I was told, "Raman has something to tell you." Curious, I waited for him to speak. What on earth would he want to say?

"I've given my life to Jesus," Raman stated deliberately.

It didn't register right away. My mouth opened and then closed. It was such a shock. I didn't think this could happen. But I was also elated. God had answered my prayer! God had used me. *He'd used me!* Now feeling responsible for nurturing my classmate, I began spending time in focused prayer, especially for Raman's spiritual well-being. Raman's conversion began a process that has deepened my Christian walk to the present day.

It was the beginning of a two-week school break. Every day I eagerly prayed and studied the Bible. Never before had I sustained this kind of activity or shown this level of spiritual hunger. But I had to know more so that I could instruct Raman and nurture him. Spiritually, I wasn't much more than a step ahead of him!

My heart surged with excitement. If Raman had become a Christian, couldn't others in our class come to know Christ as well? This was a thrilling prospect! I spent a lot of time underlining key verses in the New Testament I thought would help me. I drank in the Word of God like never before, committing a number of verses to memory. I was having my own personal revival!

When classes resumed, I'd get up at 5 A.M. to pray, read my Bible, and memorize scriptures. This was radical for me! Then at school, the witnessing started. I mainly quoted Bible verses to all comers! Although I knew nothing about the apostle Paul's method of using different approaches to invite people to become believers depending on a person's understanding of the Scriptures, I witnessed with a newfound boldness.

I bought a pocket-sized New Testament that became a prized possession. I'd even read it standing up in the streetcar as I swayed back and forth to school. At the lunch break, I'd sometimes climb the slopes of the mountain in back of our school to read and pray. New levels of understanding opened up for me all the time.

One day after school a debate asked the question, Who has served mankind more: science or religion? I had gone along just to listen. But when they asked for comments from the floor, I found myself strangely moved to rise to my feet. I felt butterflies in my stomach, and my voice betrayed my nervousness. For me to say something for God publicly was so unusual. But I was thrilled that I'd spoken out. A few days later, a boy from another class complimented me on what I'd said. I was genuinely surprised. And encouraged!

In my youthful enthusiasm, I made a number of mistakes. Like the time I used scare tactics on a classmate by showing him

Malachi 4:1 (KJV): "For, behold, the day cometh, that shall burn as an oven;…and all that do wickedly, shall be stubble: and the day that cometh shall burn them up…." And when a professing Christian in our class didn't feel like coming to the Christian meeting on campus one week, I used a similar verse on him. I shudder thinking about that today. For if salvation is loving and knowing God, there were times I sure didn't use the right approach. Thankfully, God uses us where we are while continuing to teach us.

On another occasion I tried to justify my absence from the school assembly by referring to my Christian activities. This was too much for our stern principal, who retorted, "I don't think much of your religion!" Shoulders slumped, I slowly walked back to class knowing I had not been a good Christian example.

Despite my blunders, something was happening on the inside. I was learning to share my faith, and God kept giving me opportunities to speak out for Him. But more than that, I was learning to walk with God. As a result of speaking up for the Lord, my Christian walk had dramatically changed. Raman's conversion had suddenly made the whole New Testament come alive. And praying for my classmates had similarly enlivened my prayer life!

When I heard that the debate Science versus Religion would be repeated, I felt I should be ready to say something again. This time I recruited Raman to be willing to speak, and because the debate was to be held at night, I invited Max to join us for moral support. When it came time to receive statements from the floor, all three of us participated. Summarizing the evening, the teacher in charge of the debating class referred to Max, Raman, and me negatively as the "vocal group at the back with very pronounced views!" But this did nothing to squash my growing faith. Not only had I spoken for the Lord in public again, but I had involved others! I had a growing sense that God would be giving me many more opportunities to speak on His behalf.

Learning to Speak God's Truth

Jesus impressed upon His listeners that speaking up for Him was essential to eternal life with God (Matt. 10:32–33). Although I made many mistakes when I started witnessing as a teenager, I have learned the following valuable lessons over the years.

1. *We should speak from a low, friendly position.* Any haughtiness or speaking from a high position will not attract people to God. Ultimately, our aim in witnessing is to lead people to love and know the Lord. Love is the vehicle that God uses as we witness, perhaps more than any other single method. Keep in mind that when we preach Christ, we represent the One who from the Cross forgave those who had hurt Him the most. If a loving spirit accompanies the presentation of the gospel, it validates our message. As Loren Cunningham, the founder of Youth With a Mission, says, "Truth not spoken in the spirit of Christ is untruth." The unbeliever, should he or she decide to come to Christ, would not want an arrogant Christian as a friend!

People won't always recall the *words* we speak to them, but they will usually remember *how we made them feel.* That's because we "speak" through our lives, not just our words!

2. *Use language that is understandable to non-Christians.* Every profession, organization, and religion has its own lingo or jargon, and Christianity is no exception. Using terms like *justification, redeemed,* and *born again* is not advisable for two reasons: They mean something entirely different in other walks of life, and often they're not understood at all. The story is told

of a man who saw a billboard in the United States that read, "Jesus Saves." The man honestly thought he should save his money too!

3. *Start where the listener is comfortable.* Jesus and the apostles usually presented the gospel by starting where *the listener* was comfortable. Jesus began His conversation with the woman at the well talking about water (John 4:7). When He answered the question of the expert in the law of Moses (Luke 10:25–26), He used the Mosaic law as His starting point. Starting in the area of a person's expertise makes the person relax. In Athens the apostle Paul spoke about the Greek concept of "the unknown god" before launching into the gospel (Acts 17:22–34). Notice the people who came to Christ as a result (verse 34).

It took me many years to learn how to engage a Muslim in a deeply meaningful conversation. Because Muslims believe they will go to hell if they acknowledge Jesus as God's Son, I don't open a conversation by asking, "Do you know that Jesus is the Son of God?" I usually start where we both agree (the existence of a Creator and the practice of prayer). Muslims deeply respect this approach, and I end up having long and productive conversations, even about the person of Christ. They have treated me with great hospitality, and we've parted as friends.

4. *Be sensitive to people's felt needs.* When I travel, I talk with those seated next to me on the bus or the plane or the train. Often the conversation turns to an area of their felt need: a fear of the future, a concern for their family, a sickness, or a relationship problem. People often listen intently, sometimes with tears in their eyes, because what I say hits a tender spot. Jesus ministered to felt needs when He gently dealt with such people as Zacchaeus (Luke 19:1–10), Simon Peter (Luke 5:1–11), and the woman at the well (John 4:7–19, 39), all of whom became His avid followers.

5. *Recognize the power of your testimony.* While in the Philippines recently, I took Christian young people with me as I went from classroom to classroom at a local college. We introduced ourselves as people who had messed up our lives. I described my boyhood shoplifting history while others mentioned past problems with anger or drunkenness or hatred or revealed that they'd attempted suicide. One by one we testified that Christ had changed us—that we were now different!

The combined weight of these testimonies was powerful. It showed why the gospel is indeed the "Good News." There is hope for everyone, despite the mistakes, sins, or even crimes of the past. Our testimonies also introduced these college students to a God willing to forgive. The students responded positively, asking the school administration, "When are those people coming back?" A number of them now follow the Lord and attend Christian meetings.

Don't worry if you don't have a "spectacular" testimony. Rejoice that you will have fewer potential hang-ups in your Christian life. But anyone who is a Christian will have turned from selfishness. All who are truly in Christ have that testimony.

Witnessing for Jesus is a clear command of our Lord and wonderfully demonstrates the character of God (when done in love and humility). Jesus asks us to witness because not everyone has a Bible or tunes into Christian broadcasts or wants to enter a church (a threatening place to some). We must reach people where they are.

Learning to witness for Christ gave me a whole new perspective. It turned me from living for myself and taught me to reach out to others. At the same time, it challenged me to pray meaningfully and to read the Bible more avidly. My life has not been the same since.

The somewhat lost art of personal evangelism must be rekindled. But we have to carefully represent Christ as we witness. We must be gentle and humble, yet require repentance. We must use language people understand. Perhaps what will convince people the most is a Christlike attitude and the knowledge that Jesus has changed us and can thus change them.

five

Getting the Training We Need

As I continued to share the gospel in high school, it wasn't long before I felt my life's work would be in full-time Christian ministry. I began thinking about missions. Again, there was no "heavenly vision," no trauma, no rousing meeting. Just a conviction and a desire.

I believe God's calling becomes increasingly apparent to those who seek to do His will. While He places some in education, in medicine, in business, or in other places of influence, He calls others specifically to the ministry of the Word of God (Acts 6:4; 2 Tim. 4:5). I believe He wants to call many more from this generation: young men and women who have the strength, courage, and wisdom to stand against the evils of the age and take the gospel to the ends of the earth.

About the time I felt drawn to missions, Max was taking a Spanish class. I loved languages, so I joined him in the weekly sessions. Soon I began to think of South America as a field of service. As I was finishing high school, I learned of a three-year Bible training course where I could study and work part-time to support myself. Gradually I sensed this is what I should do.

Before leaving school I filled out the required form to indicate the next step in my education. In New Zealand at that time, there was no such thing as a high school graduation. Legally a student could leave school at age fifteen. Many left after just two years of high school to enter a five-year apprenticeship in a vocation such as carpentry or electrical or mechanical engineering. Those continuing on at high school took a nationwide examination at the end of the third year. With a pass in this exam, a student could enter a teachers' or nurses' training college. Those who wanted to be doctors and lawyers stayed on in high school for yet another year.

Two hours after I'd slipped the form through the school office mail slot indicating my decision to attend Bible college, my homeroom teacher called me to the front of the classroom. He was appalled at my decision and tried to dissuade me in full view of the other students.

"Why are you going to Bible college?"

"Because I want to be a missionary," I replied.

"But why?" he asked, his eyes narrowing in disbelief. "Why waste your life when you could do so much more with your abilities?"

I had been at the top of my class for a couple of years, so I guess he thought I was throwing away my "brilliant" future. Then he continued, "Anyway, the heathen are happy."

I started to explain my reasons from the Bible, but he cut me off, replying sarcastically, "The heathen haven't heard of that!"

After twenty minutes, he told me to return to my seat. I felt I had gotten nowhere, either in convincing him about the validity of the gospel or in convincing him about the rightness of being a missionary.

I took the national exam in 1961 and scored well. Despite the opposition from my homeroom teacher, I then entered a Bible college in Hamilton, 320 miles north of Wellington. I hoped that at Bible college I would learn how to be an effective missionary and lead people to Christ. By this time, I had witnessed to scores of people, but Raman was the only one who'd come to faith. Perhaps it was my approach that scared my classmates off. I really wanted people to change, but my tactic was to persuade them by concentrating on their belief systems rather than wooing them by God's character and His depth of love for them.

I arrived in Hamilton in late summer and immediately liked its warmer climate and picturesque lake. On the first day of class, I couldn't understand how some of the studies (like the meaning of New Testament words) would ever help me lead people to Christ. But I quickly saw that the homiletics class—the art of public preaching—would be a great help. The principal was a solid biblical scholar with an understanding of how God had moved in revival. He inspired great respect, and I soon settled down and began to enjoy his teaching from the Bible, our only "textbook."

My first big spiritual lesson, however, was not learned in the lecture room. Classes were held only in the morning, which freed us to find part-time work in the afternoons or evenings. But as much as I tried, I couldn't find a job. I was staying with a church member and needed to pay for room and board as well as for school fees and other necessities. I soon exhausted the little money I had.

I had heard of Christian workers who received no salary, yet God had provided finances for them through unsolicited gifts from fellow Christians. Would God supply like that for me, a sixteen-year-old Bible student? I was extremely worried about the prospect that He wouldn't. Daily I searched the newspapers for a job and followed a number of leads. When I wasn't looking for work, I studied my notes from the morning lessons or prepared to preach in the homiletics class.

Amazingly, for the next two months, a check or money order arrived in the mail from unexpected sources without my asking for money. The finances often arrived when my resources had dwindled to almost nothing! When I finally learned not to worry about living on the edge, I landed an afternoon job laboring with a sheet metal merchant, and the flow of unsolicited money stopped. It became obvious to me that God was aware of my new circumstances!

Another out-of-class lesson came from my classmates themselves. During recess one day, a few talked about how they'd paid back what they'd stolen in their preconversion days—the biblical principle of restitution. Naturally I began to think of the articles I'd ripped off. It had never occurred to me to pay back the stores I'd stolen from.

"Where in the Bible does it say we should do that?" I asked in amazement.

"There are several places," they answered. They showed me scriptures such as Matthew 3:8 and Leviticus 6:4–5, and it was not long before I was convinced I should do the same. In my room one day I made a list of all the stores I needed to contact. One by one I wrote letters of apology. In one letter I also asked forgiveness for lying to a store owner who had suspected I'd stolen a book from his shop. He'd told me sternly, "I don't ever want to see you in this place again!"

As I worked only half a day, it took a while to mail all the letters with the appropriate-sized checks inside. I knew I was not earning my salvation. That had already been gained through the Cross. But I was putting things right with those I had clearly offended. This is what Paul meant when he said, "I strive always to keep my conscience clear before God and *man*" (Acts 24:16, emphasis added).

My presentation in the homiletics class was my first time to ever formally preach. I attempted a salvation message that was a complete disaster. Although I had put a lot of effort into its preparation, the content seemed weak when it came time to present it. Nor was I proud of my delivery. Embarrassed, I couldn't pedal away fast enough on my bicycle at the end of the morning. Slowly, over the three-year course, with the principal's skillful coaching, my public-speaking ability improved. The principal was very firm with us young men, always keen for us to improve. He particularly wanted us to give personal illustrations.

"The people listening to you preach are saying to themselves, 'How does this work?' You must prove it to them from your own life!"

At my age, that wasn't always easy, but the sense of God's call to be a missionary continued strongly. I wanted my life to count for Him. Occasionally the longing would be so great that during my third year, I'd head the old motorcycle I now owned toward a deserted beach a couple of hours from Hamilton. There at a friend's quiet cottage by the sea, I'd fast and pray all weekend. At night I'd pray and praise the Lord under the starry sky as I walked the sandy beach alone.

One night back in Hamilton, my appetite for missions was greatly stirred when a fellow student and I attended the church screening of a movie entitled *Filipino Passion*. Centered around a recent campaign in the Philippines by American evangelist T. L. Osborn, the movie showed actual footage of Filipino *flagellentes* who whipped themselves and shouldered large crosses, even allowing themselves to be nailed to the crossbeam. Though officially frowned on by the Catholic church—the predominant religion of the islands—this practice to atone for sin and to ask for divine favors still carries on to the present day.* My friend and I were so moved by the plight of those who didn't have a saving relationship with God that we told the principal we felt like leaving college.

"The world is truly going to hell!" we told him. "What are we doing here? There is so much to do now!" The principal encouraged us to stay on. I didn't really have much option. At my age, what could I do, and where would I go?

Getting the Training We Need

We all need to receive the training necessary for the calling God has placed on our lives. God calls some to be world leaders, some to be mechanics and electricians, while He calls others to be lawyers and doctors, all laboring for His glory. Those called to be church workers and missionaries need to be trained in a way appropriate for their calling too. But how and where? That is an intensely personal issue, but perhaps the following guidelines will help.

1. *Make sure the training is geared to reaching the lost.* My Bible college experience helped me accumulate academic knowledge of the Word of God while my young mind was keenly receptive. Much of the teaching I received in Bible doctrine and practical, righteous living has helped me to this day.

---

* In 1998, men dressed as Roman soldiers temporarily nailed fourteen men and one woman to a cross in a village just north of Manila.

So has the invaluable instruction in public preaching. For these, I will be forever grateful.

But the school didn't meet all my needs. It did not give me the understanding that the body of Christ must reach *every* tribe and nation according to Christ's clear statement, "And this gospel of the kingdom will be preached in the whole world as a testimony to all nations, and then the end will come" (Matt. 24:14). Whatever our calling is, it should mesh with promoting the cause of reaching the world for Jesus. That is the Church's prime mission (Mark 16:15; Luke 24:46–47). Regrettably, many Christians and even some training institutions lose sight of this central goal.

Nor did the training I received at Bible college stoke the fire in my heart for deep intercession, which is so necessary for effective evangelism. In fact, I graduated with less zeal for the lost than when I began. Looking back, it would have helped if the school had organized opportunities to go on outreaches, do street evangelism, or hold public evangelistic meetings. Later on, when I joined an energetic, evangelistic group and got more involved with people's needs, my zeal was rekindled. But I know of others who have gone through Bible college training and also lost their earlier zeal.

When Jesus came to earth, He didn't follow the Greek concept of higher education or the Jewish idea of rabbinical schools. He established no school Himself and amazingly gave no instructions to start one after He left. He was content to largely focus on twelve very ordinary men whom He trained while they watched Him listen to God, preach the gospel, heal the sick, and cast out devils. They learned through His humility, His wrestling in prayer all night, and His dealings with the hostile scribes and Pharisees. They picked up the ways of God through what He demonstrated "on the job" rather than what

He taught in an organized classroom setting. *And these disciples turned the world upside down!* All this is thought provoking, to say the very least.

Obviously, Jesus' style of teaching relied heavily on the principle of mentoring or training by example. I am so thankful to God for the mentors who helped shape my life outside the classroom over the years.

2. *Make sure the training is practical.* As I read the Gospels, I am impressed how practical Jesus' training was. Make sure the training you receive is equally useful. Jesus taught by *doing* in the following three ways.

After He had instructed His disciples, He took them *with Him.* They learned as they watched Him in action. Take the time they were in a boat on the stormy lake. When the disciples woke Jesus to calm the storm, He did so. But later He rebuked them. "Where is your faith?" He queried (Luke 8:25). He clearly wondered why they didn't act to quiet the storm themselves.

After they had traveled with Jesus, He then sent them out *alone* and had them report back. After He heard what had happened, He instructed them some more and answered the questions their "outreach" had raised. Then He sent them out again.

After three years of coaching, Jesus sent them out completely *by themselves* to teach and preach while He returned to heaven. Jesus' emphasis followed the example Ezra set: first to study, then to *do* what God says, and then to teach (see Ezra 7:10 KJV).

Given this model, are today's Bible schools and colleges relevant? I think it depends on their goals and how hands-on the training is. The apostle Paul had the equivalent of a Ph.D. from a rabbinical school and at one time taught daily "in the lecture hall of Tyrannus" (Acts 19:9). But this preaching, fasting, and praying founder of churches had a very practical emphasis.

Those closest to him as he traveled—young men like Timothy, Titus, and Tychicus—felt the greatest impact.

Unlike the teaching of the scribes and Pharisees, Jesus' emphasis was practical because it *empowered* people to fulfill the Great Commission. Avoid long, drawn-out academic programs that emphasize the retention of head knowledge to the exclusion of training to reach the lost, hear the voice of God, and expect miracles. We read that at the conclusion of Jesus' training, His "disciples went out and preached everywhere, and the Lord worked with them and confirmed his word by the signs that accompanied it" (Mark 16:20). Christ's training was both simple and effective.

3. *Make sure the objective is to share the love of God.* Recently I visited a nation where a pastor's wife lamented how those attending a local Bible training program seemed interested only in gaining knowledge. She observed that the students weren't interested in speaking to the lost on the bus as they returned home at term breaks. She compared the training program to one she had attended years before, where the students had been taught to love others and to love the unsaved.

Make sure, therefore, that the training you receive will inflame your passion to love and *serve* fellow Christians and to love and *serve* the lost. Study for that purpose, not to know more than others to lord it over them. The apostle John wrote, "Whoever lives in love lives in God..." (1 John 4:16). People will respond more to how much we *care* than what we *know*. A careful examination of Jesus' approach to one-on-one evangelism reveals that it was His caring attitude that won the woman at the well, Zacchaeus, the woman caught in adultery, and many others.

4. *Make sure the emphasis is on knowing God.* Training in the Word of God is obviously necessary for someone called to

preach. However, the emphasis in the training should always be to know the *God of the Word* as well as the written Word of God. The apostle Paul wrote that "knowledge puffs up" (1 Cor. 8:1). Even educators tell us that education can alienate us from others. Our Bible knowledge must therefore be accompanied by Christlike character.

So study the Word of God, meditate on it, and of course memorize it.* I have gained so much through memorizing and meditating on the Word of God in recent years. But more importantly, *obey* the Word. Walk it out. The Word is of little use without obedience. In Waco, Texas, in 1992, cult leader David Koresh led eighty people to their flaming deaths. He knew the information of the Bible and went around quoting it. But he certainly did not know the *God* of the Bible and definitely did not obey Him.

As someone has powerfully pointed out, you can teach what you *know*, but you only reproduce what you *are*.

---

* *He Still Speaks Today* by John Sherrill (YWAM Publishing, 1997) gives very practical reasons for memorizing and thus meditating on the Word of God.

six

Hearing the Voice of God

While at Bible college, I often struggled to discern between guidance from God and my own imagination. The process was often torturous.

I remember hitchhiking home to Wellington during a term break. There were several routes I could take, so I asked the Lord to guide me. At an important road junction, I felt directed to go by the orphanage where I'd lived for six months as a child. When I arrived I found signs of life, but not one staff person or child was at the orphanage! I left town discouraged about my ability to hear from God.

At the end of Bible college, I faced a greater need: What was God's next step for my life? Despite much prayer, I seemingly received no direction. What I subsequently did nearly torpedoed God's purposes for my life. That close shave, and the mistakes and the victories that followed, taught me much about hearing God's voice. As these principles of hearing God's voice emerged, I began to realize the connection between divine guidance and being effective in His service.

With a mild sense of awe, I stared at the letter from the headquarters of the Bank of New Zealand. I was almost afraid to open it, yet maybe its news would settle the question once and for all. I slit open the envelope and unfolded the single sheet of official stationery. After carefully reading the letter, I sighed with relief. I'd been accepted to start work at a local branch in a month's time. Finally, I knew what the foreseeable future would look like!

Two months earlier I had graduated from Bible college, but since then, no ministry opportunity had opened up. Restless, I had wondered what to do. It seemed to me I should get a decent job until it was time for me to start in full-time Christian ministry. I was almost nineteen, and to work at the bank seemed a sensible step. But doubts persisted. So I prayed that God would stop the process if it wasn't His will. I stared hard at the acceptance letter and thought, *Considering how much I've prayed, this must be His will!*

A month before I was to start work, I planned to enjoy a couple of weeks on Great Barrier Island, 150 miles northeast of Hamilton. This ruggedly beautiful island with its towering mountains once housed a whaling station in the 1800s. Even today it still has no public electricity and is a great place to get away from it all. Neville Winger, a respected Christian leader and a former board member of my Bible college, had bought a five-hundred-acre farm on the island and converted it into a permanent Christian community. I would have time to splash in the ocean, enjoy fellowship, and soak up both the sun and the rich teaching of a Christian conference.

All went well for two weeks as I enjoyed the camp activities. Lying on my bed the night before my departure, I suddenly felt a great urge to pray. I suggested this to the others in my bunkroom after the lighting from the generator had gone out. One by one we prayed. Soon, I experienced something totally new. In my mind's eye I saw a man digging a hole in the ground. I sensed he was headed for trouble. I prayed for this man so hard that I groaned as I lay on my bunk. I had never before experienced anything like this. *What on earth was going on?*

A friend from Bible college days heard my groans and ran through the darkened farmhouse to get the director. I saw the beam of a flashlight, and soon Neville, breathless from a chronic asthmatic condition, appeared at my bed.

"What's the problem, Ross?"

I sat up on the bunk and described what I had seen in my mind's eye and my strange reaction. I had been at enough prayer meetings with Neville to respect his gifts of discernment and wisdom. There was a pause, and then the voice above the flashlight said, "Ross, I sense there is a battle going on between God and the devil concerning your future. You are the man in that pit. You've gotten into a rut, and you must seek God to get out of it!"

After Neville had left the room, I lay in the eerie, dark stillness, mystified and disturbed. What could this mean? Where had I gone wrong? Could it be the job at the bank? It was a long time before I fell into a troubled sleep. By the time I awoke, the sun had peeked over the steep mountains behind the old red farmhouse. I quickly recalled the previous night's events and the boat I was scheduled to take at 8 A.M. *How could I return to the New Zealand mainland in such turmoil?*

I quickly pulled on my old clothes, grabbed my Bible, and slipped out to think and pray in a secluded spot. Of the options before me, I decided to stay on the island until I could discern what God was saying. After all, my start at the bank was still two weeks away.

After watching the small launch laden with campers slowly chug out to sea, I turned with heavy heart to walk up into the mountains to seek God. Once out of earshot, I prayed out loud, "Lord, what do you want me to do?"

If I were to give up the bank, what then? No meaningful alternatives sprang to mind. I was still considered too young to do missionary work. And no Christian ministry had opened up for me in New Zealand. I'd worried over the decision to join the bank, yet heaven had seemingly kept silent.

Clutching my Bible, I climbed the steep pastureland, sometimes scattering sheep as I walked. I hiked and prayed through the green meadows, stopping to catch my breath or read my Bible. I climbed until I could make out the coastline of the mainland far in the distance. Yet back at the old farmhouse that night, when the golden sun shimmered into the sea, I was no closer to an answer.

After two fruitless days of seeking God, I bumped into Neville.

"Ross! I need to talk to you," he said. "I read a verse in the Bible this morning that I believe is for you." I followed him to his tiny office, where he showed me Jeremiah 31:21: "Set up waymarks for yourself, make yourself guideposts; consider well the highway, the road by which you went…" (RSV). In context it meant that the Jews being exiled to Babylon were to mark the way they traveled. One day God promised He would bring them back to the land of Israel, and they would need those ancient markers. God had impressed Neville to instruct me to think of times in the past when God had spoken to *me*.

"These are signposts that will help indicate what God has for you," Neville said, pausing to use his inhaler. "Get a piece of paper and write down what you feel God has told you concerning your future. Include your inclinations and your abilities."

"It's going to be a short list," I replied.

"Try it anyway," he instructed.

I climbed the steep mountains again that day, thinking of what I could write. Sitting on lush green grass, I began jotting on a yellow legal pad, often stopping to chew on the end of my pen as I thought. To my amazement, I managed to fill the page! I listed how I'd wanted to be a missionary soon after my conversion at age fifteen; how I'd gone to Bible college; been interested in South America; found languages fascinating; and dreamed of preaching to thousands. The list went on and on. *But surely these things are in the future. I don't see how this helps now!*

I continued to seek the Lord daily in the quietness and solitude of the island. High in the hills again one day I sat on a rock in the shade of a cliff face. I riffled through my Bible until I found my place in the book of Job. Although I was reading the Bible a lot, I had little expectation that God would speak to me through my regular reading. I was in for a surprise.

My pulse quickened as I read Job 33:15–17: "In a dream, in a vision of the night, when deep sleep falleth upon men, in slumberings upon the bed; then he openeth the ears of men, and sealeth their instruction, that he may withdraw man from his purpose…" (KJV). An asterisk was beside the word *purpose*, so my eye turned to the center column of the Bible to see what the alternative meaning might be. I stared at the word given: *work*. I suddenly put it all together: to withdraw man from his work.

To withdraw me from my work!

Was God saying not to work at the bank? I sensed He was. I kept on praying and meditating and later sought out Neville. In his office I showed him the verse and all I'd written on my pad. After reading my list, he immediately said, "It's pretty clear to me!"

He could see my call to missions. So could I. But that still did not tell me what to do *now*. We talked and prayed together. As we closed, Neville looked at me intently.

"As we were praying, I had the impression you have only one year left in New Zealand." Oddly, that thought didn't frighten me.

As I continued to pray, it became clear that I should return to my parents' home in Wellington at the end of the summer. I'd get a temporary job and wait to see what God would open up for future ministry. And so I returned to Wellington and took a job laboring at a construction site. It was a perfect introduction to cross-cultural challenges. Every day I was surrounded by immigrants: South Pacific Island construction workers, Greek carpenters, and sometimes Dutch bricklayers. Only two or three others had been born in New Zealand. I was in God's "school," perfect for my missionary calling.

Many days during that winter I worked outside in the bitter cold winds, but I never regretted the decision to give up the warmth of the bank. I knew more than ever that I was called to missions. How foolish to have thought of starting a career in the bank when God had earlier given me so many spiritual signposts that pointed to missions! God had not been silent after all. *He had already been speaking to me for years through those signposts!* I was now aware that God had something around the corner for me. I could drop my present job at a moment's notice and move to wherever God led me next!

That year, I attended a church where young people conducted street meetings each Sunday afternoon. I often preached short messages after the others had testified and sung to the small crowds that had gathered. Three active members of the youth group were daughters of Dal and Dorothy Walker, missionaries home on furlough. One day when our youth group visited the Walkers' house, Dal talked with me over a hot cup of tea.

"Ross, we're leaving by ship soon for the Philippines. Once there, we'll conduct evangelistic meetings in a big tent we're taking with us. Why don't you join us for a while?"

"No way," I replied. "I'm going to South America!"

"Well, you may be," Dal replied. "But at one time I felt called to Japan. I ate, drank, and slept that vision. But it never came to pass. We've worked in Indonesia for many years and are now moving to the Philippines."

Regrettably, I didn't realize the wisdom of Dal's statement and quickly dismissed it. But kneeling by my bed in prayer a few days later, a thought suddenly gripped me. *Accept Dal's invitation to the Philippines!* It came with such suddenness and excitement that it was as if a lightbulb had been switched on in my head! Revelation came pouring in. The Philippines, like South America I'd been studying about, had experienced centuries of Spanish colonization. Wouldn't conditions be similar? I could see myself gaining valuable experience. Three months in the Philippines would be an ideal steppingstone to the future. I felt such a peace about this exciting new thought that I contacted Dal, who suggested I book my ticket for a sailing two months away.

"By that time, Ross, we'll be settled in and ready to receive you."

I had no idea what eventful months those would be. God soon tested me by asking me to give away the money I had planned to use for my trip. It was a struggle to obey this prompting, but the impression would not go away. I finally came to the conclusion that God wanted me to trust Him to miraculously supply my fare.

About this time, I heard that Neville Winger was scheduled to conduct a series of meetings in a friend's church sixty miles north in Levin. Ten months had passed since my bunkroom experience, and I was eager to tell Neville that his prediction about my having a year left in New Zealand was about to come true!

As I jammed clothes into an overnight bag that weekend, I sensed I was to buy a one-way train ticket. I was not to take any other money with me, the inner voice told me. I was to trust God to get me home. Fear suddenly gripped me. *That's just too risky!* I thought. I continued to kick those thoughts out of my mind. I felt guilty when I shoved the extra money into my wallet and when I bought a round-trip ticket at the train station.

Once in Levin I forgot all about it. I got caught up in the spirit of the meetings and fellowship with Neville and other friends. At the end of the weekend, the pastor astonished me by presenting me with a sizeable gift of money. He had no great reason, other than he was led by God, to do so! I was further surprised when an acquaintance offered to drive me back to Wellington. My immediate reaction was that of sadness. I had disobeyed God. I hadn't needed to bring money or buy a round-trip ticket. God had wanted me to enjoy the result of obeying His instruction. But I had grieved Him and spoiled the celebration for us both. I repented deeply of my disobedience. Yet out of the ashes of that failure came a redeeming lesson: The impression not to take money with me was from God. *I really was learning to hear His voice!*

In a series of remarkable incidents that taught me much about the relationship between divine guidance and stepping out in faith, God supplied for my trip to the Philippines. Money I still needed for the journey came in at the Wellington train station en route to Auckland, where I boarded the M/V *Oronsay*.*

---

* This and other faith stories are recounted in an earlier book, *Adventures in Naked Faith* by Ross Tooley (YWAM Publishing, 1996).

Two weeks later, just days after my twentieth birthday, I arrived in tropical Manila. After adjusting to the sweltering heat, the hectic traffic, and throngs of people, I traveled with the Walkers and helped with their tent campaigns. The next months were exhilarating and interesting. I witnessed on the street and sometimes preached in churches, in open places, or at a jail. One night I climbed onto the open deck of an inter-island ferry and preached the gospel through a loudspeaker system to many passengers who listened.*

After three months in the Philippines, I was invited to a small-town church in Lucban, Cagayan, in the far north of the country about four hundred miles from Manila. I didn't know it then, but when I accepted the invitation, I was in for another exciting lesson about hearing God's voice.

After almost a week of meetings, I felt God impressing me to return to Manila a day ahead of schedule. That was not a comforting thought. I didn't have the bus fare! I would have much preferred an extra day to pray in the money. God was the only one I looked to for the supply. There was no guarantee an offering would be taken for a speaker. But I couldn't shake the impression to leave early.

I took another look in my wallet. As often as I counted the bills and coins, they amounted to only three pesos (a little less than a dollar in 1966). I needed five times that amount to pay for the twenty-seven-hour bus trip over rough roads to Manila. I had only ninety minutes before the bus was to leave. I began to worry.

I made my way to my room and knelt on the wooden floor. I was still in prayer fifteen minutes later when a sudden sense of joy pierced my soul like a shaft of light bursting into a dusty

---

* Ibid.

room. I just *knew* the money would be provided. I had no further need to pray for it. The voice of God in this incident had been a "witness to my spirit," accompanied by a deep sense of peace rather than a thought that had come to my mind. I rose from my knees and clapped my hands in joy.

I glanced at my watch. The bus to take me on the first leg would pass the house in another hour. No one was aware of my need. But I *knew* I had no need to worry. Cheerfully I readied my few personal belongings.

Five minutes before the bus was due, despite the peace I'd felt earlier, I could feel the tentacles of worry begin to creep back. I made my way to the doorway. I now wondered just how far my three pesos would take me and how God would supply for the rest of the trip. Once outside, as I stopped to retie my shoes, I recognized the voice of my host.

"Here, Ross. This is for you," he said, extending a long white envelope toward me. Inside was more than twice the pesos I immediately needed!

This experience helped boost my confidence that I really was hearing God's voice. But I didn't know that a whole new series of events was shaping up just around the corner, destined by God to test and then strengthen my ability to hear His voice.

Hearing the Voice of God

Thankfully, since those struggling early days, it has become a little easier for me to hear from God as a disciple of Christ, although I still have much to learn. Over the years I have found that if I ask the following questions, the issues come into sharper focus.

1. *Are the choices before me consistent with the written Word of God?* Sometimes I immediately eliminate an option because it would go against what the Bible says.

2. *Is what I have in mind compatible with the character of God as revealed through creation and His Word?* Sometimes this stops me short. As righteous as my cause might be, I must always accomplish it in a way *consistent* with Christ's character.

3. *Do I have a settled peace in my heart (Col. 3:15)?* What sort of peace do I have? Is it a serene peace, or is it a "hope so" peace? God's peace does not leave the sort of doubt I had when I applied for the bank job. Actually, the bigger the assignment, the longer I want peace to have settled and stabilized in my heart.

4. *What are my first responsibilities?* Looking carefully at my automatic responsibilities often sorts out what is priority and what is not. My wife and family, for example, have priority over many other things.

5. *Do I have a pure motive?* It is never God's will for me to proceed if I am not motivated righteously. On the day of judgment, in my view, God will evaluate us not on the work we have done but on the reason behind our actions.

6. *Does my wife agree with this decision?* Because she will bear the consequences of my actions, it is only fair that I get her approval on any major decision. But what would happen if I weren't married? The next question becomes appropriate.

7. *Do I have the confirmation of some trusted person in the body of Christ?* We are not to be an island to ourselves. The bigger the decision we face, the greater the need to have the confirmation of a mature Christian or trusted member of the body of Christ. For me on Great Barrier Island, Neville Winger was such a person. Looking back, God used him to confirm what He had been saying to me for years!

8. *Does my decision fit in with the spiritual signposts that God has already given me?* A few years ago, decades after becoming a missionary, I was back in New Zealand enjoying a sabbatical. A nearby church was without a pastor, and I was

offered the position. Materially it was an attractive offer, as it promised a big house and a secure income. The people of that congregation, many of them getting on in years, were marvelous to us. But I turned the offer down. I am convinced that my calling right now is to teach young aspiring missionaries what I have learned through both my failures and my successes. I have learned my lesson about observing spiritual signposts.

9. *Am I being unduly swayed by circumstances?* In his book about guidance, Neville Winger writes that circumstances are one of the least reliable indicators. Circumstances, he says, are unsafe as *primary* sources of guidance but can serve as comforting confirmation. They may be used by God or molded by the devil or men. If circumstances do arrest our attention and start us thinking differently, we must go to God for confirmation.*

Too many good Christians have turned from God's original path because they think that every open door comes from heaven. They forget that a greedy businessman or even a well-meaning relative can open doors for us. The tragic story of a man of God slain by a lion because he was influenced by circumstances rather than what he had received from the Lord (1 Kings 13:15–26) gives us a striking example. Just as the contents of a prophetic message need to be evaluated (1 Cor. 14:29; 1 Thess. 5:21), opportunities need to be scrutinized to see whether they're from God.

10. *Have I been led by God to put out a "fleece," or was it my own idea?* Putting out a fleece is when we ask God for a sign, as Gideon did in Judges 6:36–40. In a sense, I did that when I prayed, "I'll apply to the bank for the job, but You stop me if this is not right." My sister, who later worked for a bank, told me they could have made leaving difficult once I'd settled in—

---

* Adapted from *Your Life, by Guess or by God* by Neville Winger (Orama Christian Fellowship, 1979). Used by permission.

such are the material benefits and incentives for promotion that they would have offered, given my abilities. What I did was almost like jumping off a roof and asking God to suspend the law of gravity if something wasn't His will! We can employ the confirmation process Gideon used, but only when led by the Holy Spirit. It is interesting that we get no examples of that process in the New Testament.

Aside from our asking these questions, God can guide us in numerous other ways. One way is through the voice of the Holy Spirit speaking directly to our hearts, such as the time He impressed me to accept Dal Walker's invitation to the Philippines.

Another form of guidance occurs when we receive a witness in our spirit, such as I received on my knees in Lucban that I didn't need to worry about my bus ticket money.

Sometimes when we read the Bible, a verse may warm itself to our hearts. Usually the verse will be doctrinally informative or will emphasize a command relevant to the situation we're facing. Occasionally, a verse will grip our hearts in such a strong way that we *know* God is talking to us directly. The portion of Scripture standing out reassures us that God knows *exactly* what we're going through and sometimes tells us what to do next. That's what happened when I read the words, "That he may withdraw man from his purpose [or work]" (Job 33:17 KJV). An occurrence of this will always be accompanied by peace and will never lead us to do anything contrary to the overall theme of the written Word of God.*

I am glad I started to learn to listen to God as a teenager. It was much easier making mistakes without involving a wife and family. And we all make mistakes. But God in His grace and

---

* See *He Still Speaks Today* by John Sherrill (YWAM Publishing, 1997, pp. 41–45) for further discussion on this aspect of hearing God's voice.

wisdom often uses our most painful mistakes (such as when I applied for the bank job) to teach us the most profound lessons (Rom. 8:28). The Bible tells us it is good for a man to bear the yoke in his youth (Lam. 3:27).

The apostle Paul wrote, "[D]o not be unwise, but understand what the will of the Lord is" (Eph. 5:17 NKJV). God meant Christianity to be a relationship, not a ritual; a real, live, warm, talking-to-each-other friendship, not a mere academic acknowledgment of His existence. Learning to hear God's voice is tied to the process of knowing God and His character and comes by our experience of walking with the Lord.

seven

The Testings of God

I was repeatedly tested during the weeks after God had provided my bus fare to Manila. That should not have surprised me. God always tests His people, just as a carpenter proves his lumber before he assembles a chair. Holding the ends of a piece of wood in his hands, the carpenter places the wood over his knee. With a jerk, he exerts pressure on it to test its strength. Once he is satisfied it will take the strain under pressure, he proceeds with his plans.

Likewise, God tests us before He gives us special assignments, and He examines us before He gives additional authority. While these times are not always pleasant, we dare not resent them. God is thinking of us. He plans to bless us as well as the world He wants us to reach.

After God tested Abraham, He was thrilled with the response and said, "Now I know that you fear God…I will surely bless you and make your descendants as numerous…as the sand on the seashore" (Gen. 22:12, 17). As a result, God made Abraham the father of a new nation. It was Abraham's descendants who gave us our Savior, the Holy Scriptures, and countless examples of heroic faith (Heb. 11:11–38).

In 1966 God desired to increase my faith, my understanding of His character, and my ability to hear His voice. Working to ready me for a career in missions, the Master Carpenter tested me to see whether I was ready.

Although it was going to be a long, hot bus journey from Lucban, Cagayan, to Manila, I was flushed with excitement as the bus bumped over pothole-covered roads. God had supplied my needs, even if it was again at the last moment. My mind turned to the young people I'd spoken to all week. I rejoiced that I'd told them about a dependable God who wanted to provide for them and use them for His glory. Their smiling faces and cheerful spirits were imprinted in my memory.

I'd enjoyed my time in the Philippines with its varied activities, including its surprises, like the time I'd been called to a church pulpit without warning and told to preach! I'd even mused and prayed over extending my stay indefinitely. But one morning in prayer, a peaceful conviction enveloped me: I was to follow my plans to return to New Zealand. Not only that, I was to trust God for an extra $320 to travel to Thailand en route to Singapore, where I'd pick up my ship home.

But $320 was a huge amount for me in those days. Especially when this twenty-seven-hour bus ride from Lucban to Manila was costing me only $6! My thoughts naturally turned to the challenge that lay ahead. When I arrived at the Walkers' home the next day, tired and thoughtful, I eagerly tore open the neat pile of envelopes that greeted me. Was this the answer to my needs? I was immediately encouraged with $112 from two faithful friends.

The test of faith continued through the next week as I obtained government clearances, made the travel arrangements, and said my good-byes. Financially I received a surprise boost when my home church in Manila took up an offering for me after I preached on Sunday night. I still didn't have enough for all my living expenses, but I now had the necessary airfares for the coming trip. As I climbed on board the Cathay Pacific flight out of Manila, I reminded myself that I would have to keep trusting God for the rest.

On arrival in Thailand with its Buddhist temples and distinctive architecture, I felt more in a foreign land than ever before. Few people spoke English, the signs in Thai script were totally incomprehensible, and the canals were busy marketplaces and transport routes. I was sobered to be in a nation that boasted more Buddhist temples than Christians.

I stayed with missionaries Paul and Bunty Collins, who had spoken briefly to our class at Bible college. That day, Paul had inspired me to believe God for the impossible, so I was glad to see him again. Paul and Bunty had set up an effective correspondence course tied to eye-catching tracts designed to be widely distributed. I handed them out on the Bangkok streets to willing Thai hands. It was so different from Wellington, where similar efforts were sometimes spurned. I rejoiced at the difference and at the opportunity to preach to young Thai Christians in a local church.

It was in Bangkok that a turn of events tested my faith and ability to hear from God more than anything I'd ever before experienced. Just before I was to fly to Singapore to board the M/V *Himalaya*, I learned that a British seamen's strike had delayed the ship's departure. At first I was not concerned. I would just stay in Bangkok a bit longer. My Thai visa could handle that.

But the strike dragged on. When I heard that the ship was held up indefinitely in London, I suddenly realized I was stranded in Bangkok! For several days I battled all sorts of fears and doubts. I had no other way to get to New Zealand and no money to retrace my steps to Manila. Why had God led me out of the Philippines? Had I stayed there, I would not be in this mess!

What was I to do now?

I could stay in Bangkok until my visa ran out, make a trip to Laos, and return on a new visa. What would I do if the strike continued? I could not stay in Thailand indefinitely.

Eventually, I felt in prayer that I should fly to Hong Kong, where I had been invited to meet with a missions director to talk about my future. I was told that I could trade my air ticket to Singapore for an air ticket to Hong Kong with the payment of an additional five dollars. In Hong Kong I would have to believe God for a ticket on to the Philippines. That would be a huge challenge, but hadn't God miraculously supplied my needs this year? Once in Manila, I'd use my boat ticket to return home. I'd just have to wait a while, as sailings were not frequent from the Philippines.

I asked the Thai travel agent to change my ticket, even though I was now down to my last thirty-five cents. God would provide the five dollars somehow. Later, I spent my last two cents on a local Bangkok bus and felt an amazing peace. That is, until the bus turned an unexpected corner and tore off into unknown territory. Now I was alarmed. I was penniless and lost amidst a bewildering array of Thai street signs. I spent what felt like eternity in panic before the bus finally stopped. Thankfully, I quickly found my bearings. Relieved, I walked the six blocks back to my bedroom at Paul and Bunty's. I immediately began to pray.

"Hallelujah, Lord," I began in faith, despite the test I found myself in. If I had known all that lay in store for me, I might not have sounded so confident. "You will provide for me. I am now without a penny. But I am a son of the living God." I continued in quiet praise for several minutes as I walked around the room.

Five minutes later, there was a knock on my door. I opened the door to receive an envelope from Paul. Inside were bright red Thai bills amounting to ten dollars!

Thank you, Lord!

Clutching the money, I excitedly walked to the travel agency while noisy motorized rickshaws zipped past and the smells of the Orient hung in the air. At the agency, I should have known something was wrong when the young woman I'd talked to earlier went to get her boss.

"Yes, well, we're very sorry," the boss said smoothly, "but we made a mistake when we quoted you five dollars. The real price is fifty-six dollars."

My heart hit my shoes. *Fifty-six dollars!* That would keep me for more than a month back in the Philippines.

"But, but…" I stammered. "You mentioned the other day…."

"I know. We're very sorry, but we made a mistake. The real price is fifty-six dollars."

I could see it wasn't any use arguing with him, but I didn't have fifty-six dollars! *What was I going to do now?* I thought of the ticket for the ship. This office had told me they couldn't refund the cost of the ticket until they'd received permission from Singapore. I asked if they'd heard word.

"No, we're sorry."

If real faith is tested faith, I was given a lesson on faith under fire that day as I walked slowly from the travel office. I began questioning everything. Was it really God who said I should now proceed to Hong Kong? And was it His will for me to come to Thailand? Had He really told me to return to New Zealand at this time? If I had extended my stay in the Philippines, I would not be having this problem!

To make things worse, I faced a physical test as well. As a result of the long, sticky, hot bus trip from Lucban to Manila three weeks earlier, I had developed an itch so painful that sometimes I couldn't sleep. Now I found myself questioning that trip as well.

I continued with a heavy heart for the next day or two. I went over and over the guidance I had received to travel to Thailand. I reminded myself of the miraculous ways in which God had previously supplied my needs. But there were still many assaults on my faith. Yet I told God that I was not mad at Him, for in the faith walk I had learned the necessity of keeping my spirit free from any bitterness.

My circumstances were like those of Joseph in Psalm 105:17–19, where the word of the Lord tested him. When God gives us instructions, I was to learn, He often tests us to see if we completely trust Him. For when we have total faith in His character, He entrusts us with even greater assignments.

Four days later the situation changed. The travel agent received permission to exchange my M/V *Himalaya* ticket for onward air travel. That did not mean a ticket back to New Zealand, but I could now fly to Hong Kong and on to Manila. I'd also have fifty-five dollars in travel credit from the ticket exchange. I was relieved that this took care of the immediate future. But it meant that I would still need to believe God for a sea ticket out of Manila.

I was soon in Hong Kong, but after two days I found myself dangerously low on finances. Worse, when my meeting with the missions director was over and I wanted to fly to Manila, all flights were sold out for over a week! *What now, Lord?*

Because I had no money to stay on at the Hong Kong YMCA, I prayed earnestly and placed myself on all standby lists that day. I also fasted. I had to. I had just enough money for a bus ticket to the airport and my departure tax. Despite the situation, it was a precious time spent in the presence of the Lord as

I clung to Him in naked faith. Before noon, however, I received a call from Philippine Airlines.

"Mr. Tooley, we can get you on a flight to Manila tonight. Will you take it?"

"Yes, I will," I answered excitedly.

"Then please bring your ticket to us for revalidation."

That news took care of one hurdle. But another obstacle immediately loomed on the horizon. How in the world would I get a new visa for the Philippines? In those days, no one entered the Philippines without a permit obtained abroad. And I didn't have the required onward ticket past Manila to get one. Worse, I didn't have money for the visa fee.

I proceeded to the airline office to at least get the ticket revalidated. Without telling the young woman behind the desk I had no money, I brought up the question of the visa.

"But I don't have an onward ticket after Manila," I told her. "All I have is this fifty-five dollar travel voucher." I told about my aborted attempt to travel on the ship and my desire to get back to friends in Manila. Suddenly she thought of something.

"May I see your passport?"

She slowly flipped over the pages, carefully examining them one by one, then stopped.

"You're okay," she said. "Your old Philippine visa is for multiple entries. You can use this again tonight." I ran my hand through my hair and sighed in relief.

When I checked out of the YMCA, I had hours to kill. With nothing else to do, I took an early bus to the Kai Tak airport. Because I had not eaten all day, I could almost smell the meal that would be served on board the airplane. But after checking in and passing through immigration, that meal was still an hour or two away. While awaiting the flight, a young Chinese woman approached me.

"Excuse me," she said politely in her accented English. "I'm from the Hong Kong Tourist Association. Could I ask some questions about your time here?"

"Sure," I replied. I had time. Too much really. I needed something to keep my mind off my hungry stomach.

"How long have you been in Hong Kong?"

"A few days."

"Could you tell me how much you spent on duty-free items?"

"Nothing."

"Did you take any tours?"

"No."

"How much did you spend on clothing?"

"Nothing."

"Would you mind telling me how much you spent on food?"

By this time I felt embarrassed. I had spent very little. Awkwardly I told her. She continued asking questions until she'd checked all the squares on her paper. That done, she looked up and smiled.

"May I buy you a snack?"

"Well, yes…Thanks very much!"

Darkness had settled over Manila by the time Philippine Airlines touched down in Manila. I couldn't call the Walkers, as they had no phone. I had nothing to cash into pesos either, but thankfully I had Philippine coins tucked away as souvenirs. They weren't enough for a taxi, so I thought of a *jeepney*, a colorful extended "jeep" into which thirteen or more people could usually squeeze. But with my traveling bags I decided against it and waited for the less frequent bus. It was therefore late when I pressed the buzzer at the Walkers' home. Although it rang repeatedly, no one responded. My heart sank yet again.

Oh no. Maybe they're on a preaching trip!

I gripped the handles on my bags once more and trudged wearily to the corner. I still had some ten *centavo* coins and managed to get both myself and my bags onto a jeepney. Arriving around midnight at my home church, it took me a while to raise a sleepy church worker, who showed me to a room for the night. As I lay down, I considered my predicament. I was back where I had begun, I had only a few small coins, and the rash was as painful as ever.

What now?

The next day I set out for the Walkers, who, I learned, had not heard the doorbell the night before. They were both surprised and happy to see me. While it was comforting to be welcomed back, I continued to wonder about my next step.

"Well, Ross, maybe you should stay around for a while. There is plenty for you to do here." The door was indeed open, and I preached my first Sunday back.

As I continued to pray over the next few days, something pulled at me telling me to return to New Zealand. That seemed odd, as it made more sense to me to stay on in the Philippines. A few days later, I felt impressed to visit missionaries Evan and Tricia Squires and wondered why. Over a meal together we reminisced about mutual friends in New Zealand, and I told them about Thailand and the seamen's strike that had forced me back. During coffee afterward, Evan suddenly surprised me with a question. "Ross, would you like to borrow some money? We have $225 saved up for our next furlough."

I was taken aback. Borrowing was not a way of life for me. I possessed no credit card and had never used a line of credit. Yet I quickly saw that if I added Evan's amount to my travel voucher, I'd have enough to buy a sea ticket home. Once back in New Zealand I'd work in construction and return the money in no time! That is, if I could get on the M/V *Aramac* due to sail on Tuesday. But then I thought of Hudson Taylor and George Müller, missionaries of bygone years whose books had inspired me. I couldn't imagine them borrowing a thing. Weakly I replied, "I'll have to think about it."

A few days later, at a time when I needed it the most, I received a check for $103 from the leader of our youth group in Wellington. It was the biggest gift I'd received all year. At the same time, I felt an increasing freedom to accept most, but not all, of the money Evan had offered. It was to be one of the few times I would borrow money in my entire missionary life.

The chances of obtaining passage on the M/V *Aramac* were slim, however. I'd tried unsuccessfully to get a booking five months earlier, but if I could secure a berth, it would confirm the pull to return to New Zealand at this time.

When the M/V *Aramac* docked on Monday, I left my passport with the travel agent, as that was a requirement for purchasing a ticket. Twice during the day I called to ask if there was a spare berth for me. Both times the agent told me the ship was sold out. Yet at the end of the day, I had the odd notion that I should take a trip to the harbor to look the ship over. After I had climbed the gangplank, a smartly outfitted officer addressed me.

"Is there something I can do for you?"

"Well, I'd hoped I could sail tomorrow," I started, "but I understand you're full. I came down to look over the ship."

"Well, mate," he said with an Australian accent, "we do have a bunk in a six-berth cabin if you're still interested." My heart skipped a beat. "You'd be sharing a cabin with five Japanese university students."

"I'll take it!"

"It's yours. But you'll need to get your ticket from our agents on shore before we leave tomorrow. Here, I'll give you their address. But make sure you're on board no later than 11 A.M. You'll miss the immigration officers otherwise."

I glanced at what he had written and thought of the extra running around I'd have to do in the morning.

It was sad telling the Walkers the news. They had introduced me to missionary life, opened doors for ministry, and treated me as a son. I felt awkward about leaving them but reminded myself I had to obey what I sensed was God's next step for me. *It would make it easier to leave if I just knew why I was supposed to return to New Zealand!*

Early the next morning I began what I thought were routine procedures to board the ship by 11 A.M. But when I arrived at the travel agency to pick up my passport, I found the office deserted. A security guard told me the employees were on strike.

"There is no way you will be able to get your passport."

Another test! Nervously I hung around, hoping someone could help me. As the time dragged on, I increasingly saw the possibility of the ship's slipping its moorings without me. But about that time, an employee I recognized walked by. He had been on the M/V *Oronsay* with me five months earlier. Eagerly I approached him and explained my predicament. He probably wasn't supposed to, but he retrieved my passport despite the strike. Clutching it gratefully, I rushed off in a taxi to the M/V *Aramac's* agents. I told myself there was still just enough time to buy the ticket, dash home for my bags, and make it to the ship.

At the M/V *Aramac's* agency, however, they quoted me a price from the wrong schedule. While their mistake was understandable, precious time ticked away as I repeatedly explained why the lower fare schedule applied to me. By the time I managed to convince them of the correct price, the deadline for boarding the ship loomed dangerously close.

At 10:40 A.M., I flew into my bedroom across town to throw last-minute items into my suitcase. Gathering my gear at the gate, I wiped perspiration from my brow as I hailed a taxi, then said hasty farewells to the Walkers.

I looked at my watch several times during that taxi ride while my stomach churned. Reaching the ship late, I managed to clamber on board before the immigration officers went off duty. It was hardly a relaxing way to leave. But as the ship steamed out of the bay and I climbed on deck, I looked back at the skyline of Manila with gratitude that God had intervened yet again.

Postscript

As the M/V *Aramac* sailed out of Manila, I was unaware that the other ship, the M/V *Himalaya*, had not docked in Singapore after the strike ended. I learned much later that in an effort to make up time, it had sailed directly to Australia from the Suez Canal. A wait in Thailand would have been in vain. Even if I had followed my original schedule and stayed safely in the Philippines, I could not have sailed with the M/V *Himalaya* as planned. God had a purpose for my going to Bangkok and Hong Kong, but He had guided me safely back to the Philippines.

The M/V *Aramac* captain set a southerly course to pass through the islands en route to Australia. With my heart firmly fixed on South America, I could never have anticipated what God had in store for me: that in these very Philippine islands I would work with teams of young people for thirteen years. As I leaned against the rail and looked in the direction of Thailand, I didn't know I'd spend months in evangelism in that country or carry Bibles into China from Hong Kong. And as we sailed past the northern Indonesian island of Celebes a week later, I had no idea what high adventure lay in store for me on that island in years to come. I didn't know I would spend a third of a century as a missionary in the Asia and Pacific region.

I did believe that what God had led me into over the past five months would help me in my future ministry. I would also realize the value of the testings to hear God's voice. Those experiences proved invaluable as I later challenged young people to step out in evangelism and trust God for their finances.

During the two-week voyage home, I figured my life would be predictable for the next few months. My rash had cleared up, and after this relaxing trip on board, I'd work hard in construction to pay Evan back. But in just a few days, on board this very ship, I would learn why God was calling me back to New Zealand.

The Testings of God

While God's ways are always the best, they aren't always the easiest. When things don't go our way, we sometimes forget that God is working behind the scenes.

When we Christians stand before the judgment seat of Christ (2 Cor. 5:10), it won't be our earthly treasures that matter. Of utmost importance will be how our character developed and what we learned of God's ways while on earth. These spiritual assets are often learned through hardships and testings. Just as an expensive pearl comes into existence as a result of an oyster's irritation, so can spiritual blessing flow through difficulties.

Over the years, the Old Testament story of Joseph has been an inspiration to me. God shaped his servant Joseph—who was sold into slavery by jealous brothers and thrown into prison for refusing to compromise his sexual purity—on the anvil of affliction. Later, when starving people appealed to Pharaoh for food, the king of Egypt stretched out his arm and said, "Go to Joseph…" (Gen. 41:55). If we are prepared to obey God and suffer for His name, God will send the spiritually hungry our way, for He'll know we'll feed them with the knowledge of God and His ways.

After forty years of being prepared in the backside of the desert, Moses was thrust into confrontation after confrontation with a stubborn Pharaoh. Even when God miraculously delivered Israel, Moses had to constantly put up with his people's bickering and complaining. But his response to trials turned him into the most humble man of his era (Num. 12:3). Thousands of years later, I am inspired when I read about his humility, obedience, and ability to hear from God.

Christianity calls us to place *knowing God and His ways* far above the world's drive for gratification. We are to take the higher route and do what God asks us to do. Obedience to Him sometimes means being asked to do the unusual. If that happens, we should take that as a mark of God's confidence in us. And if God calls us to a career in missions, He will test us to see whether we'll go the distance.

During our testings we often beg God to remove the difficulties. Perhaps we would get through our trials faster, however, if instead we asked God what He wanted us to learn through the experience. Recently while going through a time of bewildering circumstances, I found that spiritual exercise to be thoroughly comforting.

On the other hand, testings can stretch over months or years. And when a trial is obviously God-given, we are to submit to it. If we keep our attitudes right, the reward to the body of Christ through our lives will be far greater than any hardships we might have experienced (2 Cor. 4:17). Fiery times have not always been easy for me, but afterward they took my love for God soaring to new heights!

I vividly remember the illustration Bob Mumford gave of watching a monarch butterfly emerge from a cocoon. The process of struggle was so painful to watch that Mumford slit the shell open with his pocket knife. Unaware that struggling from a cocoon is God's way of forcing fluid from the butterfly's body into the wings, Mumford's act resulted in disaster. The butterfly flopped out with a beautiful wing on one side and a useless blob on the other. The exquisite insect would never fly. The point is clear: If we short-circuit a God-given trial, we risk emerging useless.

To the Western youth of today, it may seem strange that struggle should even exist in God's kingdom. We have so much affluence that we are spiritually poverty-stricken as a result. We have instant meals, instant entertainment, and instant fast cash from credit cards. Regrettably, many feel they should have instant sex, drugs, and MTV as well. Some young people have their own cars, cell phones, and seventy-channel TV sets to watch. Yet the incidence of depression and attempted suicide among youth is increasing at an alarming rate (up 300 percent since the 1960s). So are school violence, apathy, and the use of antidepressant drugs. Affluence (or the welfare state) has not cured the ills of our society. Struggle prepares us better for life than do riches.

If trials are a necessary part of the Christian life, are there ways to guide us through these times? Bible teacher Joy Dawson recommends we keep ourselves in the written Word of God and in worship. She also urges the study of the character of God as a way of life. Of her own fiery trial with relentless back pain for five years as a result of surgery, she says, "My faith would have failed had I not taken much time to study the character of God *as a way of life.* I had nothing else to cling to or hang my faith on."

The testings of God are a necessary part of a Christian's journey to spiritual maturity. Luke 4:1 states, "Jesus...was led by the Spirit in the desert." A desert, of course, is a barren place where very little grows. Yet the Holy Spirit thrust Jesus into that burning wasteland where Jesus fasted, prayed, and wrestled with the devil himself. If we want to be like Jesus and return "in the power of the Spirit" (Luke 4:14), we must also be prepared to be "led by the Spirit in the desert." The two go together.

eight

Fulfilling Our Ministry

It's one thing to know your ministry calling, but quite another to start living it out. It had been my observation that young preachers didn't have much opportunity in New Zealand. I had spoken in a regular church meeting only once before going to the Philippines. While my missionary journey gave me more experience and confidence, I did not expect New Zealand churches to give me—a twenty-year-old—much opportunity once back home.

I soon learned that God's call on my life meant God's enabling. God simply wanted me to respond to my calling with faith and obedience. He then opened doors beyond my wildest expectations. It all started with a revelation I received in prayer while on the high seas sailing from the Philippines. Then came the challenge of discipleship: to lovingly follow the directions He gave.

The smiling Japanese students bowed slightly as I entered the cabin for the first time on board the M/V *Aramac* as it set sail from Manila. They introduced themselves as students of a "floating university" on board. They often spoke in Japanese, making me feel I was in the land of Mount Fuji. Even on this trip home, the Lord was exposing me to more Asian culture, but with my eyes so fixed on South America, I didn't see what He was doing.

One morning while alone in the cabin, several days into the two-week sea voyage, I dropped to my knees to spend an extended time with the Lord. I read the Bible for a while and then gently pushed it to one side to pray. God's choice of a job once I arrived home was uppermost on my mind. I needed to repay Evan and Tricia as soon as possible.

I hadn't been praying long when I sensed a gentle inner voice begin to speak: *I have not called you from a land you loved, where you were needed and where you experienced blessing, just to have you bury yourself in a job in Wellington. You are to get out and speak for Me, creating a missionary vision in both young and old alike.*

I leaned back on my knees for a few seconds, struck by the thought's strong logic. Of course! Why else would God take me from a productive time in the Philippines? Just then an opposing thought crashed over me like a huge wave. *How would I get the money back to Evan?* I'd have to believe God for His supply beyond my traveling needs. *I'd have to be sure of that!* Evan and Tricia needed the money for their furlough later in the year.

For the rest of the voyage I was often in deep thought. As I leaned over the ship's rail, smelled the salty spray, and watched the white foam dance below me, I wondered about traveling around New Zealand as a twenty-year-old. I pondered the word that had come to me while on my knees in the cabin: *You are to get out and speak for the Lord.* Up to now, my adventures in faith had mostly affected me. But if I messed up in this next step, Evan and Tricia would be adversely affected. If it's really God's will to promote missions like this, I thought, I'll need to have a deep peace about it.

By the time I reached Wellington, with its beautiful harbor and familiar hills, such a peace had settled in my heart. I knew I was to spread the missionary vision and trust God to supply my needs. I still wondered how I'd get invited to speak at anything more than a handful of prayer meetings. In 1966 people my age did not go on short-term missionary trips, and they certainly did not travel around promoting missions! However, I immediately began sharing my adventures and showed slides to Mom and Dad and other family members and any others who would watch and listen.

Wellington in winter was cold after the heat of the tropics, but at the end of the first week, I enjoyed warm fellowship in a prayer meeting in the home of the copastor of our church. I respected the wit and friendliness of Pastor Trevor Chandler, whose spiritual fervor and giftings had earned him wide respect. Pastor Chandler asked me to talk about my trip before the group prayed. I felt honored and in broad strokes quickly painted a picture of the work in the Philippines and shared how God had miraculously supplied my needs. Then we all prayed.

About half an hour into the prayer time, I heard Pastor Chandler pray out loud for me and felt his hand on my shoulder as I knelt in prayer. Then he spoke directly to me: "I see a picture of a hand holding a book," he began. "You are not to hide yourself. You are not to hide your voice. You are to boldly go forth!"

I remained on my knees in reverent awe. God was confirming publicly what He had said to me privately in the M/V *Aramac* cabin. I took the open book to mean the Bible. The rest meant that I was not to "hide" in a job but that I was to travel and talk and preach, encouraging people into missions. A wonderful peace descended on me.

Still on my knees, I thought of the church in Levin, where, shortly before going to the Philippines, I'd heard Neville Winger speak. Pastor Ken Read had given me a monetary gift, which had been a great encouragement when I'd been in need. I figured that he and my other friends in that town would welcome a visit.

"Okay, Lord," I prayed quietly, "after the Sunday morning service in Wellington, I will start out for Levin."

On arrival at the evening meeting in Levin, I noticed a 16-mm projector set up in the small sanctuary and recognized Al Erickson, a warm-hearted Canadian who showed gospel films throughout New Zealand. Al and Pastor Read pumped my hand in friendly greeting.

"I'd love to have you testify about your time in the Philippines," Pastor Read said with a smile. "Could you do it halfway through the film show, before Al starts the second reel?"

I was delighted at the opportunity to fill in the time between reels and enthusiastically gave a report when the moment arrived. At the end of the meeting, I helped Al with the movie equipment. His Canadian-accented English suddenly broke through my thoughts.

"Say, Ross. How about traveling with me to Wanganui tomorrow, eh? You could testify again at the changing of the reels."

"Sure, I'd love to," I replied. "But where would I stay?"

"I'm sure we'll find a bed for you!"

The next day I enjoyed chatting with Al as we drove north through the lush green dairy-farming region. That night when my turn came to speak, I looked out over a crowd I'd never seen before. I guess it was because of my boyish appearance that they looked at me inquisitively, but I didn't let it bother me. I relived my six months abroad, referring to the tent campaigns and the times I'd openly shared the Lord and led people in prayer to receive Christ. I excitedly shared how God had miraculously provided my needs. At the end of the meeting, I once more helped Al break down the equipment.

"Say, Ross. Tomorrow I'm going farther north. Would you like to come with me and do the same as you did tonight?"

After that third meeting, Al asked me if I would accompany him to yet a fourth town, farther north in the province of Taranaki. The next day he had an even bigger surprise for me.

"Say, Ross," he started out in his now familiar Canadian twang. "Next month I'm going to the South Island. I'll put this van on the overnight ferry and then drive to the very south of the island. I'll take meetings down there for three weeks. Would you like to come along?"

I could hardly believe my ears! The whole idea of getting the vision out in the unfamiliar territory of the South Island appealed to me.

"Well…," I stammered, "I'll need to pray about it. But yes, I sure am interested…."

"You'll need to get your own ticket for the ferry both ways. It would be great to have your company!"

By now Al had reached the turnaround point of his northern itinerary. So the next day I hopped on a bus to Hamilton, where I had attended Bible college. I stayed with my good friends Bern and Joyce Pomeroy, who told me that the Orama campground on Great Barrier Island currently ran a rehabilitation program. One day, Mrs. Pomeroy approached me with a twinkle in her eye.

"Ross, how would you like to fly to Great Barrier Island at our expense? I'm sure your friends on staff would like to see you." Again, I was stunned by their generous invitation, which I gratefully accepted. After all, the trip to the South Island was still three weeks away.

Returning to Orama, where God had spoken to me in the past, sent my spirit soaring. Neville Winger was not on the island, but other friends welcomed me warmly and invited me to speak both mornings and evenings to the group of young people in residence. God was opening up even more speaking opportunities!

When I wasn't speaking or preparing my messages, I sometimes bundled myself up in winter clothing and walked the mountain trails I knew so well. I basked in the joy of all that God had done since the time I'd been on the brink of taking the bank job eighteen months before. One day I found the huge rock at the top of the steep meadow where I had read the Bible passage that had changed the direction of my life. Deep in thought, I slowly found my way down the steep slopes to the farmhouse. What if I'd not hearkened to God's call? I would have missed out on so much! Grateful to God for His grace, I returned to the farmhouse, where I continued to preach and recount my Asian adventures. Finally it was time to leave on the seaplane, which bounced wildly over the swells of the sea before taking off.

Two speaking engagements opened up in cities north of Wellington, and then it was time to link up with Al for the trip to the South Island. It was another close-shave experience for me. Someone unaware that I didn't have the finances for the boat fare handed me money the day the ferry sailed. I excitedly clambered on board the overnight ferry, where Al went over his plan with me.

"When we get off the ship tomorrow," he said, "we'll begin to travel all the way down to the bottom of the island. We'll call on pastors in whose churches we'll hold meetings on the way back."

Many of the pastors were of the same denomination as Dal and Dorothy Walker. As I was introduced, some of them told me they'd read an article I'd written about my time preaching on top of a ship's hold while at sea between the islands of the Philippines. I was surprised to hear Al encouraging these pastors to book me for youth services, and it became apparent that I would have a separate itinerary for the trip home.

One Saturday night, I preached at a youth gathering in a wind-swept coastal town on Foveaux Strait, where the prevailing southerlies from Antarctica left trees permanently leaning away from the ocean. I was about as far away from Wellington as one could go and still be in New Zealand. I spoke from the story of seventeen-year-old Joseph in Genesis 37, declaring that God calls young people to His service. At the same time, Joseph's trials shaped his life so that God could use him at a later date. To illustrate, I shared the difficulties and pressure times I'd experienced in Thailand, Hong Kong, and elsewhere. In attendance was Pastor Kindah Greening from nearby Invercargill. Having lost a child several months before, he was moved by the message and asked me to speak to his church the very next night.

After that engagement I realized I was down to just four cents. I clearly lacked the means to fulfill the forthcoming engagements that had been set up for me, let alone have enough money to catch the ferry to Wellington. *Or pay back Evan.* Before I left Invercargill, however, Kindah surprised me with a gift that provided for my immediate traveling expenses.

As I waved good-bye, I could not have known how often I would see Kindah over the next several years. From his church alone, six young people would move out into short-term missions as a direct result of my efforts. Some of them would later enter full-time Christian ministry. They would get their start through a channel I would introduce that I didn't yet know about. This was a pity, because, as happy as I was doing this work, I was stymied in one important area. As I gave my best pitch for missions, I had no avenue through which to send young men and women to the mission field.

After three weeks, I returned to Wellington overwhelmed with the excitement of what God was doing. I'd traveled extensively and seen Him supply the traveling expenses—which in itself was a miracle.

After spending time with my family, I headed north and once again watched in quiet wonder at the ministry doors God opened. A pastor in the city of Rotorua took me to different forestry townships, where night after night I was the main speaker. By this time, I was preaching at Sunday morning meetings. God had certainly opened amazing doors!

But now I had to make a major decision. Although more ministry was opening up, I had to face the fact that after three months of traveling the country, I had been able to return only a small portion of Evan's money. Should I keep on preaching and trust God for the finances or find employment? I decided to return to Wellington to do temporary construction work. I was convinced that God would open up my overseas ministry before long.

Just a few days before the deadline for returning the balance of what I owed to Evan, I still didn't have most of it. The situation threw my mind back to all the other experiences I'd had in trusting God for money over the past twelve months. It was nerve-wracking.

One night as I returned home from the construction site, my mom handed me an envelope that bore no return address. Tearing it open, I stared for a long time at a money order from an anonymous donor. It was for more than the amount I owed Evan!

That gift was a cause for great rejoicing. But in moments of quiet reflection afterward, I realized that God had supplied the money without help from my construction job. What would have happened if I'd continued traveling and ministered in Auckland, New Zealand's largest city? That question still haunts me.

As I continued in construction, a strong conviction gripped my heart that I was to quit my job at Christmas, just six weeks away, and travel to Great Barrier Island for one of its conferences. I had no idea why, but I felt particularly impressed to attend the second conference, which would start after New Year's.

About this time, the senior pastor of our church in Wellington flew in from a world trip. One night he enthusiastically told us about his evangelistic meetings in the Philippines with Dal Walker, a trip I'd helped set up. As he related story after story, something stirred deep within me. I left the meeting aching to be back in that kind of work again.

As the year drew to a close, I eagerly looked forward to the conference and the Southern Hemisphere summer. The day finally arrived when I stepped onto the wooden pier at Great Barrier Island to be greeted by my friend Graham Read from Levin. Before he took the ship back to the mainland, he drew me aside. I could tell by the tone of his voice he had something important to say.

"There are some Americans at the conference you should listen to. I think you will be very interested in their plans and what they have to say."

These visitors had come to introduce a youth program to New Zealand called Youth With A Mission (YWAM), which I had never heard of. At first I was not attracted to their plan to take young people to evangelize in the South Pacific islands. I was far too set on South America for that.

A few days later, Loren Cunningham, the founder of YWAM, arrived to speak in support of his program. I took a liking to this thirty-one-year-old Californian and his friendly ways. One night we sat together at the supper table in the big conference tent, and I told him of my interest in South America. As the sun began to sink behind the tall Norfolk pines at the water's edge, Loren eagerly drew a map of the continent and began to outline his vision for that part of the world.

"We're about to send a pilot team into Latin America, and there is one place left in our van which is to leave shortly. I'll call Los Angeles and reserve a place for you if you feel that seat is for you!"

I could hardly believe my ears. This seemed to be the opening I was waiting for! I immediately threw myself into prayer, and over the next few days, I walked Great Barrier Island's familiar mountain trails under the warm summer sun.

Despite my excitement and all my praying, the solid sense of peace needed for such a venture did not come. Later I learned that the van never left Los Angeles. God had directed me to that second conference not to send me to South America but to link me to YWAM, which I joined that same month, January 1967.

Postscript

I have continued to serve with Youth With A Mission since that time. YWAM proved to be the avenue through which most youth I recruited got into missions. Also, I hadn't any idea that my route through New Zealand in 1966 would become an important future preaching course that I would use often as I recruited for YWAM. I would introduce YWAMers Barry Austin and then Dean Sherman to this circuit in the next two years. As a result of the recruiting trips with these gifted men, young people from varied walks of life embarked on short-term and long-term missions. They would include those who would one day be pastors, missionaries, and well-known YWAM leaders who've made significant marks on their world.

Fulfilling Our Ministry

The apostle Paul wrote: "See to it that you complete the work you have received in the Lord." I believe there are several keys to successfully fulfilling our ministry.

1. *We should be aware of the importance of a consistent prayer life.* I would have been lost without the direction I received in prayer. As Andrew Murray once said, "There has never been a man or woman of God who has not been a man or woman of prayer." If we plan to be used by God, prayer will always play a major role in our lives. Jesus' teaching on the necessity of persistent prayer (Luke 11:5–13; 18:1–8) and His own prayer life (Mark 1:35–37; Luke 6:12) give us no leeway to think otherwise. The examples of Moses, Samuel, and Daniel in the Old Testament and the leadership of the early Church serve to confirm this (Acts 1:14; 13:2–3).

2. *We need to keep ourselves immersed in the Word of God.* Recently as I was memorizing the first Psalm, I was struck by the thought that God wants us to meditate day and night in His law, or commandments. Keeping ourselves engrossed in His Word and His directives for our lives is far more important than chasing after the latest movie or video release. One will lead us to be

prosperous in our work for the Lord and inspire our faith in God's character (Psa. 1:3). The other can tend to drag us down spiritually and inspire us to acquire worldly tendencies.

3. *We must allow God to develop our character.* Loren Cunningham teaches, "If we take care of the development of our character, God will take care of the scope of our ministry." The reasons are easy to see. The higher a tree grows, the more violent the opposition from the wind and other elements. Hence, a tree's roots must be correspondingly deep to withstand these forces. In the same way, the more we are used of the Lord, the more deeply rooted in God we must be to withstand the opposition the devil hurls at us. A disciple is not to despise the dealings of the Lord as He shapes us for useful service (Heb. 12:5–11). If our hearts are set on God's glory, we should expect God to discipline us and rein us in when we are arrogant, rebellious, or unforgiving. God does not promote what will work against His glory.

4. *We must learn the importance of obedience to God.* He will often hold back further ministry guidance if we have not done the last thing He asked us to do. He loves us too much to do otherwise. We must also stay true to our calling. We cannot bargain with God, such as saying we'll make big money for His work if He will change His mind about our being a preacher. Nor should we venture off to minister to Amazon tribes if He wants us to be a medical doctor in downtown New York.

What if we *have* disobeyed God? In the railroad world before the invention of cranes, if a locomotive left the tracks, it was pulled straight back along the path it used after it jumped the rails. If we have gone astray, we should go back to the point where we deviated from God's purpose and repent openly, as I had to when He revealed the bank was not for me. We should then do the next thing He says. Sometimes, when circumstances have drastically changed, He will give us something *new* to do. But to hear what to do next, we as Christians must first repent (Rev. 2:4–5). The key to continually walking with God is to do *the next thing He asks us to do.*

Like the skilled horticulturist who attends to rare plants, we are to watch over the call of God on our lives. The Scriptures clearly warn us that the fulfillment of that call doesn't happen automatically. The priest Eli is a sad example of a man of great promise who failed to live up to God's expectations. God removed both Eli and his sons from the priesthood because of disobedience, when it had earlier been the intention of God to use Eli's house forever (1 Sam. 2:30–35). King Saul is another painful illustration of a man destined for greatness who did not reach the heights God expected (1 Sam. 10:1 cp, 1 Sam. 15:23b).

5. *We should allow God to choose mentors for us who will be examples of righteousness, intercession, and hearing God's voice.* Neville Winger, Pastor Chandler, and Dal and Dorothy Walker were such people to me at a young age. At the same time, the biographies of Hudson Taylor, Rees Howell, and George Müller spoke deeply into my life. Later in my ministry came Loren Cunningham, Floyd McClung, and Joy Dawson, who were visible models for me to emulate. Mentors are people in whom God places a special love for us. What makes them distinct is that they *believe* in us.

In His justice, God provides those who believe in us, for Jesus said, "[N]o one who has left home…for me and the gospel will fail to receive a hundred times as much in this present age (homes, brothers, sisters, mothers, children…) and in the age to come, eternal life" (Mark 10:29–30). We all need to have people who love and affirm us. Ask the Lord to raise up the right mentors for you.

Sometimes we don't always get the full revelation about our life's work when we think we need it. Some ask how I ended up in mission work in Asia and the Pacific rather than South America, when I had felt drawn toward that part of the world for so long. The Bible says, "For we know in part and we prophesy in part" (1 Cor. 13:9). I believe that we also get guidance in part, sometimes getting only one piece of the jigsaw puzzle of our future at a time.

From God's perspective, the important thing was for me to be prepared for missionary work, as that is my calling. Once I was ready, it was relatively easy for God to adjust my geographical direction. So long as I was geared to go to South America, I could stay focused on missions and on important issues, such as not dating anyone who was not also called to missions. After all these years, I am not disappointed that God ultimately called me to Asia.

As far as the call of God is concerned, there is a part that only God can do: to choose the role we play in His vineyard. There is also a part that only we can fulfill: to trust and obey, which will open doors for us. If we will do our part, He will surely do His and supply all we need spiritually, morally, and physically.

nine

Finding Our Life's Partner

Not everyone is called to be married. But for those who are, few decisions in life are more important than selecting a marriage partner. Vibrant young Christians through the ages have had their ministries neutralized by marrying someone who didn't share their life's goals or with whom they weren't spiritually compatible.

I can't say it was a smooth road finding my partner or that I've had the perfect marriage. But thirty years later, I'm glad that I set myself certain guidelines and that God led me in the choice. It would otherwise have been difficult fulfilling my calling in God.

Finding a husband or wife doesn't occur in a vacuum, and for a Christian worker, it obviously happens in the context of the work of the Lord. When I found my future wife, God showed me how much could be accomplished for Him through our combined lives long before we tied the knot.

S oon after I met Loren Cunningham, I began spreading the vision of Youth With A Mission among the churches where I had previously spoken. Later, I joined a YWAM team that witnessed in the South Pacific nations of Fiji, New Caledonia, and Vanuatu. Upon my return, I showed slides and recruited in meetings throughout New Zealand. At the end of my South Island trip, I was about to book myself on the overnight ferry to Wellington when an odd thought slipped into my mind: *Take the plane and not the ship.* It was certainly a strange idea, for I had never flown that sector before. I had never before had the money to. This time though, amazingly, I could afford to fly, yet I was in no hurry. So insistent was the thought that I should fly, however, that I bought an air ticket and arrived in Wellington a whole day ahead of schedule.

Still on the lookout for opportunities to share about the South Pacific, I called a Christian leader I knew named Brian Caughley, whose youth meeting met that very night. Brian immediately invited me to speak.

"You'll preach for thirty minutes. Then we'll break for tea and coffee before going into a time of intercession."

I gave my South Pacific report and started enthusiastically into my message. I'd been speaking five minutes when I noticed two young women walk in and take a seat at the back. One of them immediately caught my eye. She was a beautiful brunette, but it wasn't just her physical attractiveness that caught my attention. It was as if God had said, "This young woman knows Me in a very real way." Nothing more. The thought of speaking to her or pursuing her didn't even enter my mind. I kept on preaching.

Concerned about French-speaking New Caledonia and Vanuatu, I asked the thirty young people if they had learned that language. The young woman with the dark hair raised her hand. In case she was a good YWAM prospect, I figured I should talk to her. It was that and no more.

During the refreshment break, I struck up a conversation with the young woman, who I learned was named Margaret Keys. I couldn't help noticing how tastefully dressed and well-spoken she was. We talked about the French-speaking islands in the Pacific, and then the topic turned to Thailand, where a friend of hers had just gone to do mission work. In turn I told Margaret about my trip to Bangkok the previous year and mentioned the photos I'd taken. The more we talked, the more my interest in this young woman began to rise.

After the break, we sat together for the spirited time of corporate prayer. So as not to appear too eager, I fell into conversation with the person seated on the other side of me when the prayer meeting ended. Later, I looked around for Margaret. She was gone. *Oh well, what a pity!* I chatted with someone else for a few minutes and then on a whim found myself opening the main door to see whether Margaret might still be outside. To my surprise, I found her on a step just a few feet away.

"Back home I have those pictures I took in Thailand," I offered. "Could we get together sometime?" I could hardly believe my boldness. I couldn't see us getting together romantically, yet something was urging me to seek her out.

"Well, yes," she replied politely, "let me give you my work phone number." After jotting down the number, she explained, "I work in an architect's office at the Wellington Railway Station. You'll need to ask for this extension."

I looked at the number she had written in flawless hand-writing and then said good-bye. As I rode the bus home, it was hard to keep her from my thoughts. *There is absolutely no way this could develop into anything,* I told myself. *But, she is such a lovely girl!*

Once home, I decided to leave the next day for an extended prayer time in a friend's seaside cottage seventy miles away. I'd been promoting a YWAM trip to the South Pacific kingdom of Tonga but still wasn't sure whether I should join the group. If I went, I'd need to prepare myself spiritually. I'd also need to believe God for the airfare and the ground fees. I decided to hitchhike to the beach house from the railroad station at the edge of town.

As I took the city bus to the railroad station, my thoughts turned to the young woman I'd met the night before. I called Margaret from the railroad station to say I'd be unable to show her the Thailand pictures until the end of the week. That done, I told her where I was. It was the sort of thing you say just to make conversation. There was no way we could see each other at this time of day.

"Oh, well," she started. "Coffee break is late this morning. I can come down. Where exactly are you?"

I couldn't believe my ears!

Margaret soon appeared, and we talked nonstop while seated on a bench just a few feet from passengers in line to buy train tickets. Some of the talk centered around Tonga. By now I was really interested in this young woman. I had always been shy around girls, but an unusual boldness came over me.

"I'd really like us to see each other again."

"Oh. Well...when you get back, please contact me," Margaret replied politely but thoughtfully. "I'll give you my home telephone number." I was carefully putting the piece of paper in my pocket when she sweetly asked, "Shall we pray before you leave?" Her kind face framed by her dark hair looked at me expectantly.

"Well, yes," I replied without hesitating. Inside I was impressed that she would suggest this in full view of everyone. *This is quite a girl!* We bowed our heads and prayed for a few glorious minutes before standing to shake hands.

When I emerged from the train station, my heart was swirling. I didn't know it then, but Margaret had meant that I should contact her after my proposed trip to *Tonga*. But as I began to thumb a lift out of town, I figured I'd contact her in Wellington at the end of that week!

I prayed and fasted for most of my three days at the cottage, often taking long walks along the deserted beach to pour out my soul to God in praise or to pray for my future ministry. At twenty-one years of age, I had few responsibilities, so I could unhurriedly commune with God day or night. I spent long periods in His Word, taking notes as I read. My focus was to find out whether I should venture on this trip to Tonga, and I eventually sensed a settled peace about it. But every now and again, I also found myself seriously praying about one Margaret Keys!

Before I returned to Wellington, I traveled to nearby Palmerston North to visit Al Hunt, the pastor who'd let me use the seaside cottage. Mrs. Hunt welcomed me, and I soon was drinking a cup of steaming hot tea at the table in the warmth of her kitchen. She looked at me intently.

"I was making the bed recently when I received a real burden to pray for you. It was so intense, I began weeping and cried out to God for you!" I felt moved by the kind expression on her face. "Can you remember what you were doing at 11 A.M. Monday morning a week ago?"

I thought for a moment and then replied. "Yes, I was on board a plane from the South Island to Wellington." I tried to put it all together. It was the day I had taken the unusual step of flying home and had preached in Wellington instead of sleeping on an overnight ferry. I told Mrs. Hunt about the message I'd given. But as I swallowed the last of my tea, I wondered whether meeting Margaret had something to do with Mrs. Hunt's special time of prayer. Later I learned that Margaret rarely attended that meeting and had appeared only because her two regular piano students had one by one mysteriously canceled their lessons.

That weekend I showed Margaret the pictures from Thailand before we attended church together. A few days later when I again left Wellington, Margaret stepped out of her office at the train station to see me off. We shook hands before I boarded the overnight train to Auckland, where I'd take the flight to Fiji and then to Tonga.

I still didn't have the finances for the trip to Tonga, and of course, had no idea how God would supply them. But I was in for a surprise the next morning. My brother Max met the train during a whistle stop at a station close to where he now lived. In the predawn darkness, he found my carriage and handed me an envelope just before the train pulled out of the station. As the train gathered speed, I ripped open the envelope to find a check big enough to pay for the trip to Tonga! I leaned back in my seat, touched by the kindness of Max and his wife, Anna, and overwhelmed once more at God's perfect timing.

That night I was on the jet to Fiji with the group. A few days later we landed in Tonga. As our small DC-3 propeller plane taxied along the grass tarmac near rows of swaying coconut palms, I could scarcely have imagined the adventures that lay ahead in this island kingdom.

Early in the outreach, crowds from the surrounding Tongan villages and islands poured into the capital city of Nuku'alofa to celebrate the coronation of King Taufa'ahau Toupou IV, who succeeded his revered mother, the late Queen Salote. We seized the opportunity to evangelize both from house to house and in the street. Then at night, as many as four groups of us preached the gospel simultaneously in the main part of town. We attracted crowds first by singing. Then we testified and preached and sang again until 11 P.M. We regularly gave our listeners the opportunity to declare their intention to follow Christ in a new way. Many answered the call.

Faithful young Tongan born-again Christians, dressed in their wraparound *lavalavas*, worked energetically beside us preaching, interpreting, or giving their testimonies. It was such a thrill that I would have preferred to have preached beyond the 11 P.M. cutoff time!

Although Margaret and I often corresponded, it wasn't until much later that I learned how important her intercession was to the success of our ministry. On the night of July 4, 1967, a fireworks display from an American naval vessel lit up the sky to the *oohs* and *aahs* of the crowd who watched from the beach. I couldn't help noticing a sea of dark-haired islanders stretched as far as the eye could see in the semidarkness. Whereas I had thrilled at the size of the gatherings we'd preached to on the main street, I'd never seen a crowd this size anywhere in my South Pacific travels. What an opportunity! *When this fireworks display comes to an end,* I thought, *we should preach.* This opportunity would never present itself again!

As the last red, blue, and white lights faded from the exploding skyrockets, I turned to my fellow YWAMers and excitedly called out, "Let's sing!" This was my signal that we should start a street meeting.

Taking a deep breath, I began to sing loudly. The other team members joined in rather than let me sing a solo, and in a few minutes a large crowd encircled us. Seeing a flagpole just yards from the beach, I jumped up on the dais and began to preach. I exhorted the crowd to turn from all that they knew was wrong and give their lives to Jesus. "If any man is in Christ," I excitedly announced with a flourish of hand gestures, "he is a new creation. Old things have passed away and everything becomes new!"

About ten minutes later, I called for a response, and several people stepped from the crowd as an act of giving their lives to Christ. Among our group was Dean Sherman, a red-headed youth pastor who had joined us from the United States. I encouraged Dean to continue the preaching while I counseled those who had stepped forward. After several rounds of preaching, with many coming to Christ, our little group of YWAMers joyfully returned to the church hall, where we all slept on the floor.

I didn't know that in New Zealand, Margaret had felt so strongly to pray for the outreach that she'd given up practicing for a prestigious piano examination. When I heard that, I couldn't help feel that her prayers had had a lot to do with the remarkable times we had. God was already using our relationship for the extension of His kingdom.

After the coronation of the Tongan king, fourteen of us young men from the YWAM team crowded onto a sixty-foot sailboat already loaded with seventy-five islanders. We sailed through seas so choppy that I soon threw up from seasickness, but by the time the sky darkened into night, all discomfort had gone. Like everyone else, I curled up on the open deck under the stars and fell asleep. Finally, late on the second day, we glided into a port of the Ha'apai group of islands.

The trip was worth the agony. Soon after our arrival at an island without even one car for its dirt roads, we thrilled to see most of the students of a high school come to Christ through the team's efforts. The principal saw the difference Christ had made to her school. A few weeks later she told us, "Mondays were always a headache, for on that day the teachers brought reports of all the students' wrongdoing. But now, all I get are accounts of a few girls being late." She added with a contented smile, "I even find *ripe* bananas in the school garden. This is unheard of!"

The prayers of relatives of the mission participants and church people were proving very effective. So, too, I figured later, were those offered by Margaret. In one letter, she wrote of her desire to meet an authority on intercession named Joy Dawson, who then lived in Auckland, New Zealand. Things were happening in Margaret's life of intercession that she needed advice on. I immediately sent her Joy's address and encouraged her to ask for an appointment. But prayer wasn't the only thing that occupied Margaret's day. She was an avid follower of current affairs and wanted me to know what was happening in the rest of the world. One day on this little island measuring only one mile by five miles, a boat brought in three copies of *Time* magazine that Margaret had airmailed to Nuku'alofa. I was deeply moved by her act of kindness expressed by the expense that she had incurred.

Later in the outreach, three of us sailed to a northern island group called Vava'u, where astonishingly we saw a move of God in a high school similar to what we'd seen in Ha'apai. I enjoyed seeing God at work, and I continued to send letters off to the young woman back in New Zealand who was intently praying for us.

All too soon the outreach was over. I would have loved to have stayed on, but my ticket could not be changed. By letter I had previously invited Margaret to visit Auckland after I arrived back in New Zealand so that she could meet with Joy Dawson. We would both stay with Max and Anna for a weekend. After two months of solid letter writing, a friendship based on shared spiritual values had begun to blossom.

On the Saturday night after I arrived back in New Zealand, Margaret and I chatted together as we zipped along an Auckland freeway in Max's car en route to the appointment with Joy. When we reached downtown Auckland, I pulled off the freeway and drove to the Teen Challenge center coffee bar located in a basement next to a nightclub. We descended the stairs and asked for Joy Dawson.

At the beginning of my life of faith, Joy had been mightily used of God to release me from crippling unbelief. I was confident she would have much to share with Margaret. I knocked on the door I'd been directed to. That done, I left the two women alone.

Later, as we began the drive back to Max's, I expected a lively time of conversation and warm friendship. But Margaret seemed distant and cold. She seemed to sit as far away from me as possible. We drove the twenty-five miles in almost total silence.

The next morning, Margaret accompanied me to a church where I preached, and then that night I drove her to the train station for her return to Wellington. As the guard blew the whistle, we again shook hands. For me, the weekend had been a great disappointment.

When I arrived in Wellington a week later, Margaret was back to her normal cheery self. She explained what had happened at the Teen Challenge center. "As soon as Joy closed the door behind us, she asked me what I was doing with you. She strongly cautioned me to make absolutely sure our relationship was God's will. She said she knew the hand of God was strongly upon you. I had so much of the fear of God on me that I didn't even want to talk to you coming home that night!"

I felt my jaw sag. I had no idea Joy felt so strongly about my spiritual walk. Although I felt encouraged on that score, I felt miffed that her comments had come between Margaret and me. Later, however, I realized that what Joy had said made total sense. *If we were meant for each other, it wouldn't hurt to be sure about it.* Ironically, I was to find out later that soon after our time in Auckland, God had given Margaret a confirmation about our relationship.

As I continued to travel and recruit for YWAM throughout New Zealand, our friendship grew through letter writing and my visits home to Wellington. Margaret and I talked about our future together. I could see that we were spiritually compatible. We both wanted to serve the Lord as missionaries, but I really wanted to make sure that marriage was God's will for us on two counts. First, I had previously "felt sure" about someone else. Although I remained friends with that person, the relationship hadn't worked out as I had thought it would. This had left me confused.

Second, there was the question of timing. After all, I had to approach Margaret's dad and ask his permission. I hadn't spent much time with Mr. Keys, but Margaret had said that when he first heard of me, he had not been impressed. He was an engineer with a top government post and a good salary. I was a preacher with no guaranteed means of income. In those days, I often took young New Zealanders door-to-door sharing the gospel. Mr. and Mrs. Keys were not evangelical Christians and did not understand this kind of activity. They were unhappy about the prospect of our being missionaries. His response without even meeting me was, "Definitely not!"

This seemed to me a huge obstacle. In those days, to get married in New Zealand, a woman under twenty-one, as Margaret was, needed both parents' approval. The question of my having no guaranteed means of support came up one night after supper at the Keyses' home. I was standing beside Mrs. Keys in the lounge when she launched into a speech about the difficulties of life without a secure income. Suddenly I found myself saying, "But can God fail?"

Mrs. Keys looked uneasy. As a churchgoer, she didn't want to say yes, but at the same time she was very uncomfortable with my trusting God for finances. The conversation turned to other things.

At the end of that year, Margaret and I joined a YWAM outreach to the Fijian Islands led by my friend Dean Sherman. In Fiji, we took advantage of the duty-free shopping and bought an engagement ring. Margaret couldn't wear it yet, but we were sure the day would come.

Because of the nature of the outreach, we saw little of each other until the last day. In any event, our relationship had always been marked by the fact that we didn't want it to interfere with the call of God on our lives. We were to worship God, not the relationship. All too soon, Margaret boarded the tiny plane with other members of the team. I waved good-bye and watched until the plane became a little dot in the sky. It would be three months before we'd see each other again.

Dean and I witnessed in Fiji for a few more weeks and then moved on to the French-speaking islands of New Caledonia, where we worked with a local church. It was while I was doing what God had laid on my heart that I received an unexpected boost. Loren Cunningham and his wife, Darlene, visited Wellington and at Margaret's invitation stayed at the Keyses' home. Mrs. Keys was so impressed with the couple's winning ways and their ability to travel while living by faith that her opposition to our marriage simply evaporated! I was disappointed to hear that Mr. Keys had been out of town at such a crucial time!

After New Caledonia, Dean and I traveled throughout New Zealand recruiting for YWAM in many of the churches God had opened up for me previously. Whenever we preached in Wellington, Margaret joined us and testified of her time in Fiji, where Indians had burned their Hindu images as they turned to Christ. Again, God was using our relationship for His glory.

This particular recruiting time came to an end when Dean moved to Sydney to be Australia's first resident YWAMer. Meanwhile, I shifted to Auckland to assume leadership of YWAM in New Zealand. Margaret and I now lived four hundred miles apart. And so I waited. Even when Margaret's older sister Janet encouraged me to talk to her father, I still didn't make a move, as I had no leading from God to approach him. Months went by.

In late 1968, almost a year and a half after we had met, I was traveling to Wellington for a long weekend when suddenly I felt God's peace. Now was the time to approach Mr. Keys. I had only a few dollars to my name. *Ah, well,* I said thoughtfully to myself, *God knows best!*

At the beach the next day I told Margaret. The glorious brightness of the summer day matched our feelings. We hugged and excitedly talked about our lives together. The coming months would be busy for us both, especially for me, as I'd prepare for and lead the next outreach to the South Pacific. We worked out a wedding date to propose to Margaret's parents: April the following year, a full five months away. I would be twenty-three and Margaret twenty.

The next day Margaret arranged to have her mom invite me for lunch so that I could talk to her dad. As I approached their house, I mused on the fact that I had only two dollars, should he ask, "How much money do you have, young man?" God had arranged for yet another step of faith for me to take.

Margaret and I had worked out a little strategy. After lunch, I'd walk with her dad to the lounge and ask the question. At least that was the plan. But Mr. Keys got wind of it. Instead of heading for the lounge as he usually did, he deliberately started to wash the dishes. I threw a glance at Margaret, wondering what I should do. Privy to our plan, Mrs. Keys spoke to her husband.

"Les, I'll take care of those!"

"It's all right," he replied politely, almost fearfully from his self-appointed post. "I'll do them!"

I stood there awkwardly, pondering my options. Finally I pulled myself up to all of my six feet two inches and towered over him. "Excuse me, Mr. Keys, but I would like to talk to you."

He looked up meekly and said, "Okay," as if he had been caught. Turning to his wife, he said, "You come with me, dear!"

Once in the lounge, Mr. Keys slid the kitchen door closed behind him. But if he thought he'd stop his daughters from listening, he was mistaken. I learned later that both Margaret and Janet had knelt by the door to eavesdrop.

After Mr. Keys took a seat, I came straight to the point.

"Margaret and I would love to get married."

"What are you going to live on, and where?"

"We will be living in the house in Auckland where YWAM pays the rent." This was absolutely true, although at that precise moment I was the only full-time worker in YWAM New Zealand. My friend Dean Sherman was the only full-time YWAMer in Australia. In 1968 YWAM was still a small organization.

For the next ten minutes the focus of conversation was the YWAM house in Auckland where I lived. Then Mr. Keys suddenly switched gears and zeroed in on Margaret's piano.

"Margaret needs that piano," he said, looking at the upright behind me. His next statement was to give me a lot of hope.

"I'll get the railroad to freight it up to you." He said it so quietly, yet it was like a trumpet sound to me. It was his signal that he was not going to oppose the marriage. I gave Mr. and Mrs. Keys our suggested date for the wedding—April 19, 1969. They agreed. Nothing more was said about what we would live on. I didn't have to reveal that I had only two dollars in my pocket! (I had no money in the bank, no car, no furniture, no material possessions other than my clothes and a few Christian books!)

Margaret brought out the engagement ring we'd bought in Fiji. Mrs. Keys was totally amazed that there'd been a diamond ring in her house for almost a year! In the kitchen with the others present, I lovingly placed the ring on Margaret's finger and kissed her. We were finally engaged!

The next five months were busy months. With only the assistance of some part-time help, I organized the entire outreach to Fiji over the long Southern Hemisphere Christmas/summer break for forty-six New Zealanders. When Dean Sherman and a group from Australia arrived, a total of fifty-four of us witnessed and preached for six weeks down the west coast of Fiji's biggest island. Margaret and I saw relatively little of each other during the outreach.

When I arrived back in Wellington for the wedding, only the first night of our honeymoon had been paid for. Once again I had only a few dollars in my pocket. As Margaret walked down the aisle toward me, she looked absolutely gorgeous. My mind was so taken up with the importance and excitement of the ceremony that there was no time to think about something as mundane as money. I knew that God would supply our needs. And He did. Along with the wedding gifts came gifts of cash thoughtfully placed in wedding cards. With that money we paid for our ten-day honeymoon in the far north of New Zealand. God even provided ten days of glorious weather!

Finding Our Life's Partner

A good marriage, they say, is made in heaven. But it's the choices we make on earth that determine how heavenly our marriage will be. The bottom line, of course, is that a marriage must be of God to succeed spiritually. But how do we know it is really God's will to marry someone? We can ask ourselves a few questions that will narrow the field to help us assess what is God's will on this important matter.

1. *Is the other person a Christian?* Of utmost importance is obedience to the written Word of God, which states that we are to marry only those in the Christian faith (1 Cor. 7:39; 9:5; 2 Cor. 6:14). When we disobey, disastrous consequences almost inevitably result. I once heard that when a Christian marries a non-Christian with the noble intention of bringing his or her spouse to the Lord, that objective is not realized 90 percent of the time. Worse, in 70 percent of the cases, it is the non-Christian who prevails and *leads the Christian astray,* either away from the Lord or from going to church. Or both.

2. *Are we spiritually compatible?* Marriage was never meant to be a student/teacher relationship, with one spouse more spiritually mature than the other. Each spouse needs to be able to encourage and speak into the life of the other spouse. Strain can develop in a marriage if the same partner always inspires, encourages, and hears from God.

3. *Is the call of God on our lives compatible?* If he is called to be a lawyer in East Los Angeles to help the poor and needy and she is called to be a missionary in Mongolia, the callings are not compatible. As a young man, I couldn't see how I could marry

anyone not called to full-time Christian service. It wouldn't be fair to the Lord, to her, or to me.

Above all these considerations, obviously, is the need to know that God has *brought the partners together* (Matt. 19:6). Even then, the *timing* has to be right, as the story of this chapter illustrates. Margaret and I waited almost two years for the right time. Often God has things in our lives to work on before we are ready to take on the responsibilities of marriage.

Because marriage usually leads to children, it is important that couples be ready for that responsibility. Rearing a child requires both partners to possess a certain amount of wholeness. Healthy questions a couple should ask are, "Are we getting married because we need it or because we want to serve God through our marriage?" and "Is our primary concern the glory of God or our own happiness?" The Bible does not say, "Seek first the pursuit of happiness," but rather, "Seek first the kingdom of God…and all these things shall be added to you" (Matt. 6:33 NKJV). Marriage is not just a license for sex, for example.

An essential ingredient of wholeness is the ability to forgive. People who can't forgive should not even think of marrying. Two *good* forgivers are needed for one good marriage.

Who we marry will determine the scope and effectiveness of our ministry and how well (or badly) we fulfill the call of God. Our marriage will mold the destiny of our children and grandchildren and descendants for generations to come. It will shape the way we deal with our children as teenagers and with important problems such as middle age and menopause later in life. Marriage will also determine who our in-laws will be and whether they will bless us or drag us down. Because of all the above, a good maxim to consider when contemplating marriage is, "If in doubt, don't." As our Bible college principal taught us, "If you wait for God's time, you will get God's best!"

How about the dating process itself? How much affection should be shown to each other before marriage? Do Scripture and the character of God give us boundaries? The answer is a definite yes! It is wrong to deliberately arouse feelings that cannot be righteously fulfilled. This is called lasciviousness or lewdness in the Bible. Jesus spoke against it (Mark 7:22), as did the apostles (2 Cor. 12:21; 1 Peter 4:3; Jude 4). In addition, Scripture clearly forbids sexual intercourse before marriage (1 Cor. 6:9–10; Gal. 5:19–21; Rev. 21:8). It explains that the wrath of God comes on those who are disobedient in this area (Eph. 5:5; Heb. 13:4).

That last statement may raise the eyebrows of some, but consider the following possible consequences of sexual intercourse before marriage from which a God dedicated to our well-being wishes to spare us: sexually transmitted diseases (including AIDS), unwanted pregnancy, debilitating guilt, the loss of a sense of self-worth, and the loss of trust between each other (if your partner yielded unrighteously before marriage, couldn't he or she yield to someone else at a time of temptation *after* marriage?). The seeds of mistrust—dangerous to any marriage—will have already been planted.

It is not that God wants to *limit* our fun. Indeed, He wants to *multiply* it. A counselor once told me that the greatest problem he had encountered in listening to marriage problems was when the young couple had engaged in sexual relations before they married. "This becomes a point of bitterness later on that smolders and smolders," he explained. "In some cases, it can even lead to the breakup of the marriage."

So, how far should a couple go in showing affection? Perhaps the greatest piece of advice I have heard comes from Joy Dawson, who teaches, "You should ask for the fear of God to be upon you as you spend time together and go no further than the fear of God allows." Margaret and I did not engage in premarital sex. And if I had my life over again, I would not want to even kiss my wife until we were married. Kissing is like lighting the fuse wire to a bomb. It is much easier to stop the first feelings than to stamp out all those that follow. Recently I took part in a wedding ceremony where the bride and groom kissed for the first time. I believe the loud applause was partly for the stand this popular young American couple took. They had not let Hollywood brainwash them!

The Emotional Architect of the universe rejoices over marriage. After all, He thought it up. But we will find fulfillment in marriage only as we follow His blueprint for our lives. That means we are to let God choose our husband or wife, and we are to treat our spouse with *agape* love—the kind of love that serves others with no thought of receiving in return. God abundantly demonstrated that kind of love when He sent Jesus to earth. In miniature, every marriage is supposed to be a picture of God's love for His people (Eph. 5:24–25).

A final consideration: How should we balance Christian ministry with being newly married? Some lay their ministry down for twelve months on the basis of Deuteronomy 24:5, which forbids going to war for a year after marriage. I would counsel against that line of thinking. The first year of marriage should be free of *hectic* ministry to be sure. There should also be adequate privacy. But I can't think of a faster way to atrophy spiritually than to give up a concern for the lost and Christian ministry and just concentrate on married pleasures.

Moses spoke of one person putting a *thousand* to flight with God's help. But two! *Two* can send *ten thousand* fleeing (Deut. 32:30)! God ordained marriage for His glory. If we submit our marriage plans to Him, He will greatly broaden our ability to extend His kingdom.

ten

Walking by Faith

Faith is essential in the life of a disciple. We all need to exercise it to obey God, to put aside fear, or to overcome temptation. Faith is believing in God's great character to the extent that we trust Him no matter what. No wonder Bible heroes were commended for their faith, for through it they conquered kingdoms, administered justice, gained what was promised, shut up the mouths of lions, or were tortured because they refused to disobey God (Heb. 11:33–35). Faith is not optional for a follower of Jesus. The Bible tells us that we cannot please the Lord without it (Heb. 11:6).

How then can we increase our faith? I believe that if we believe God's Word, our faith strengthens, and if we fail to trust God, our faith weakens. I have also learned that a loving God wants to continually take our faith to new and higher levels if we will just allow Him. Eighteen months after we were married, He gave Margaret and me this opportunity. It was an important assignment, and I will always remember the spiritual lessons that accompanied it.

Zea

After our honeymoon, Margaret and I lived in the YWAM house not far from downtown Auckland. The neighborhood, with its once grand Victorian-style houses, was now in a state of decay. To many, it was no longer a desirable place to live, but that didn't bother us. Young people easily found our central location and collected literature about our outreaches. We shopped downtown and spoke in churches all over the lively, cosmopolitan city. Besides, we were in love with the Lord, His work, and each other. From this house we traveled the country, taught evangelism, and recruited young people for our evangelistic outreaches while two recently recruited secretaries worked the office.

A large part of our work involved leading young people into practical evangelism, which in those days meant going from house to house. Through the efforts of these youth, God touched lives in vital ways. At one door, my partner and I met a young woman who invited us in as if she'd been waiting for us. As we talked, we learned that her husband had just abandoned her and her two little girls.

"I've been so miserable," the woman told us, "that I've thought of pouring gasoline through this house and consigning us all to the flames." With hearts stirred, we sat in her living room and eagerly told her how much Christ could change her. About an hour later, we led her to peace with God and the start of a brand-new life. Many of the teams of young people who went door to door returned excitedly with their own stories to share.

At year's end, Margaret and I led a team of thirty-five New anders to evangelize in a wide area of the Indonesian island of Java. At the end of the outreach, when the teams returned to New Zealand, Margaret and I moved on to join a group traveling in Asia with YWAM leader Floyd McClung. We witnessed for Christ day after day and taught evangelism in Thailand, Sri Lanka, India, and Singapore. A highlight for me was witnessing to a bank manager while cashing traveler's checks and then leading him to the Lord a week later. We are good friends to this day.

Those nine months in Asia as a young married couple inspired us. We sensed that God was calling us to return to this region. Slowly, the vision to lead a yearlong "Around Asia" team grew in our hearts. We talked over plans. I thrilled at the thought of team members remaining in Asia to work for the Lord once that outreach was over. We returned to New Zealand to recruit and assemble such a team.

Once back in Auckland, we drove to Wellington to see our families and then held meetings in many cities. As a result of our efforts, we received eleven applications, even one from Pastor Kindah Greening's church in faraway Invercargill.

God provided for our immediate needs as we traveled and preached. But we wondered how we would pay for the coming fourteen-month trip around Asia. Since we still needed three thousand dollars for airfares and ground fees, it was natural to think of selling the few things we possessed: our washing machine and refrigerator and the piano. But it became a conviction to give them away and trust God for His provision.

I also felt we should give a sizeable gift to Joy Dawson for her trip from Auckland to Switzerland, where she would teach in YWAM's first training school. Wanting to make the gift anonymous, I bought a money order. But over the next month, Joy figured out whose handwriting was on the envelope and called to thank me! She asked about our needs and promised to pray that God would provide for us.

Our meager supply was further depleted when I visited the tax department and ended up with our biggest tax bill to date, a bill that with hindsight we should never have had to pay. But God was using these events to teach me more of His ways. As the day of departure drew closer and closer, we realized we needed a miracle. No one knew of our huge financial need except Joy Dawson.

Just a few days before our intended departure, Margaret's mother and father arrived from Wellington. Although they didn't stay with us, the ever practical Mr. Keys helped us pack our missionary barrels. As wonderful as this was, I couldn't help but groan inside that my parents-in-law were around at the time I needed the biggest amount of money ever. *Oh, boy! What would happen if our money doesn't come in?* With Mr. and Mrs. Keyses' past worries about our finances, a delay would be extremely embarrassing. And how would we face the team we'd assembled?

The departure day dawned with us still lacking eight hundred dollars in airline ticket money alone, a small fortune for us in 1970. We had nothing, of course, for ground fees. I arose early and walked to a nearby park in the cool of the early hour. I found a bench under a tree and immediately started to pray. Our flight would take off at 2 P.M. We needed that eight hundred dollars in just six hours!

I thought of the people who'd be at the airport that afternoon. We'd worked with many young people during our outreaches over the past two years, and a small army of Christians had said they'd see us off. This would be a major farewell, as we didn't know when we'd be back. I wondered what Mr. and Mrs. Keys would say if we couldn't travel.

As I prayed on that park bench, a thought popped into my mind from nowhere: *You are going to look like a real big fool when you get to the airport this afternoon and you don't have the money to fly. What will your parents-in-law and all your friends think of you then?*

Thankfully, in just a second or two, I recognized the evil source of the voice. By the grace of God, I found myself rebuking the enemy. "I don't care, Satan!" I snapped. "Even if no money comes in and I'm humbled at that airport, I want you to know we are doing what God told us to do!"

I was surprised at the words that tumbled out of my mouth. Where had I received that insight? Was this bold faith the result of Joy's intercession? I learned a lesson in that difficult situation I have never forgotten: Faith and humility go together. As strenuous as the situation was, Margaret and I were to obey God and leave the consequences to Him. That settled, I walked home.

We had breakfast as planned and worked on last-minute packing. I calculated that the latest time I could pay for our tickets downtown was 11:30 A.M. I'd still have enough time to check in if I drove straight from the inner city. Margaret's parents had arranged to drive her to the airport.

Having served with us in New Zealand, Fiji, and Indonesia, Brian Caughley, the young man who'd led the meeting where Margaret and I first met, had now joined Youth With A Mission. Because Brian was about to take my place as the YWAM New Zealand director, we talked over last-minute details. Every time the phone rang or someone knocked at the door, I wondered if our financial deliverance had arrived. It was difficult to keep my mind fully on the task at hand. By the ominous hour of 11:30, however, nothing had changed.

The only thing I knew to do was to check our post office box en route to the airline office. Our missionary barrels were stacked at the wharf, and Margaret's parents had taken our suitcases to the airport. This was the last possible moment for God to supply.

Thinking he was now aware of our crisis, I asked Brian to come with me just as Jesus had wanted His disciples to be with Him at a time of need. As I stopped at the first set of lights, my heart was in my mouth. As I drummed my fingertips nervously on the steering wheel, I mentioned to Brian how historic this adventure would be. As we continued to talk, it suddenly dawned on me that Brian had not been aware of our financial plight until this point. Soon we reached the harbor, with its blue-green waters, at the bottom of Queen Street, and I pulled into a parking stall near the post office. Making our way to the box, I inserted the key as I had hundreds of times before. With butterflies in my stomach, I opened the box and cautiously peered inside.

Except for fliers and invoices, nothing! With a sinking heart, I quietly closed the box and breathed out, "What do we do now?"

After a moment or two, Brian asked, "How much do you still need, Ross?"

"Eight hundred dollars."

That was what we still needed just for airfares. I said nothing about ground fees for the next fourteen months. Brian thought for a moment.

"I could loan you eight hundred dollars."

I immediately felt uneasy. Thinking he was aware of our situation, I had asked him to come with me for moral support, not to play on his sympathies. I had no idea he had this kind of money to loan. I leaned against the wall, stared at the rows of postal boxes, and breathed out a sigh. It was a tempting offer. I thought of all the people about to drive to the airport to see us off, not to mention my parents-in-law. But the test had already been passed on the park bench earlier that morning.

I felt no peace about accepting Brian's very kind offer and mentioned my reluctance to him. God would have to supply the money we needed. I felt empty and numb. Soon I heard Brian's voice break into my thoughts.

"Then I'll give you eight hundred dollars."

New emotions now swirled within me. *I didn't accept his offer of a loan, so he feels obligated to give me the money!* I was really embarrassed.

"Brother, are you sure?"

"Yes," he said quietly and confidently.

We discussed the situation for a minute or two. I glanced at my watch. It was 11:45 A.M. The plane would take off in just over two hours from the other side of the metropolis, and I didn't have a ticket yet! If I was going to make the plane, we had better get moving.

"Thanks, Brian. Thanks so much!"

We quickly threaded our way through the heavy pedestrian traffic toward the airline office only a block away. I was known at this ticket office where I'd booked groups before, and an older female clerk greeted me warmly. As I sat at her desk, a warm glow of peace and relief enveloped me. I wished I could call Margaret, but she was en route to the airport. What would be going through the mind of this wonderful wife God had given me? She didn't know whether we would make the plane or not. A few minutes later, my mind was jerked back to the airline office as the agent stood to dramatically place two sets of tickets into my hands.

We had no time to waste. We returned to the car and hurried to the airport, managing to arrive in good time. Well-wishers could be seen dotted around the airport. Margaret came up to me and asked sweetly, "Are we going?"

It would have been appropriate to sweep her into my arms or for us to dance a jig together. But as her parents would not have understood or approved of our way of doing things, I quietly brought her up to date, and then I announced, "I'll take all the bags and check in for us both. You can stay here to talk to those who've come to see us off."

This was a big farewell, as we were making a major move to live in Southeast Asia. We didn't know then that it would be ten years (and three children) later before we'd again visit New Zealand together. Nor did we know what years of joy and high adventure lay ahead of us.

After checking in, I brought Jim and Joy Dawson up to date. It was Joy's victory as much as anyone's. She had continued to intercede until the last moment for us. As we said our good-byes, my mind was more on the miracle of God's provision than anything else. We still didn't have our ground fees, but my faith was sky-high. The God who had supplied the needs of today would also provide for tomorrow.

All too soon we boarded the Air New Zealand plane and buckled up. At the end of the tarmac, the pilot released the brakes and the DC-8 jet roared down the runway. Now with all the details taken care of, I suddenly realized the enormity of what had happened. As we lifted off, I thought to myself, *If I ever believed in a miracle-working God, it is today!*

Three hours later, we landed in Australia and were greeted by the cheery sight of Trevor Chandler, who now pastored a Brisbane church. During this overnight stopover, Trevor had arranged for us to speak. We enjoyed meeting his congregation, who in turn generously gave us a love offering. When the Philippine Airlines flight took off the next morning, we had the money to cover the first month of ground fees. A week later, when our team from New Zealand caught up with us in Manila, they handed me a note from Brian Caughley. After slitting the envelope open, I read, "After you left, someone gave me eight hundred dollars, the exact amount I gave you." Pleased with that turn of events I read on. I could hardly believe the words on the page before me: "Trish and I feel before God we are to pass this on for your travels around Asia. We'll send it on after it's been processed."

Postscript

It's a principle in God that blessing follows testing (Luke 4:1–13; Acts 16:23–30). We certainly had much to praise Him for during those fourteen months of witnessing, teaching, and preaching in various Asian nations. Only eternity will reveal all the good that was accomplished. It became obvious to me that God had placed His hand on the trip to develop the lives of us all. Eight of us continued in full-time Christian work. Kel Steiner and Mike Shelling were used of God in the Philippines, as was Diane Hawke (now Campbell) in Singapore. Twenty-nine years later, Val Bateup is still a missionary in Thailand faithfully working among the country's children and youth. Mike Webster did missionary service in Botswana for several years, while Bruce Wast pastors in a major New Zealand city today. After the fourteen-month tour ended, Margaret and I stayed in the Philippines for twelve unforgettable years.

Walking by Faith

Of utmost importance to God is the growth of our faith in His character. Christ placed much emphasis on faith and was disappointed when He didn't see it in His early disciples (Matt. 14:30–31; 17:17; Mark 6:6; 16:14). The disciples recognized their lack, so one day they requested Jesus to rectify it (Luke 17:5).

Jesus replied that even if their faith was as small as the size of a mustard seed, they could believe for a mulberry tree to be miraculously uprooted. Perhaps Jesus meant that they were to use the faith they already had before they could expect it to increase. Or perhaps He wanted to emphasize how wrong it was to not use the little faith they *already* had. Because the Bible says a measure of faith is given to all (Rom. 12:3), we must therefore exercise it. Faith is like a muscle. It has to be used in order to grow.

But what is faith *really*?

We exercise biblical faith whenever we believe a *promise* God has given us. Yet faith is grounded in something even deeper than God's pledge to us. It is rooted in *His character*. It is only because of God's integrity that we can hang on to His promises. (How many of us have been disappointed in a friend's unfulfilled assurances because of weakness in his or her character?) God has no such defect. Faith therefore declares that God can be trusted. That is why Jesus was disturbed when people failed to believe God.

This is why humility also plays such a vital part in faith. If we are more intent on proudly protecting our image instead of God's glory and character, faith will be impossible. Even today, when I am faced with difficulties, I sometimes use the thought that came to me on the park bench—"I am simply doing what God told me to do!" That principle also helps me when I am worried about what people think of me.

In John 5:44, Jesus asked the Pharisees, "How can you believe [in Me] if you accept praise from one another...?" The answer is simple. They couldn't. If we are going to have faith in Jesus, we may be subject to ridicule. In such cases, we'll need to say, "If there is a price to pay, I am going to have to pay it!"

Most of us suffer very little for exercising our faith. Consider the three Hebrews thrown into the blazing furnace because they refused to worship the image King Nebuchadnezzar set up. Their stand was exemplary. "God...is able to save us," they declared. "But even if He does not...we will not serve your gods..." (Dan. 3:17–18). We all know God did save them—not *from* the furnace but *in* it.

Consider the test faced by young Cassie Bernall in the 1999 school shooting in Colorado. When the two gunmen burst into the Columbine High School library and asked whether anyone believed in Christ, seventeen-year-old Cassie spoke up. With the barrel of a gun poked in her face, the question was repeated. Again she replied yes and lost her life as a consequence. Inspired by that heroism, many have come to Christ or have started to follow Him more fully. Faith, then, is doing what God asks us to do and being willing to face the consequences.

The following are the principles of faith by which our ministry is governed, "carved," as it were, from our understanding of the Word of God and the experiences through which we have passed.

1. *We must receive God's guidance before we launch out in faith.* Otherwise, we are walking in presumption. The apostle Peter made sure he had a "word" from God before he even took one step out of the boat to miraculously walk on the water (Matt. 14:28–29). The Bible says that faith comes by hearing the Word of God, or by hearing a message from God (Rom. 10:17).

2. *We must not abandon what God tells us.* Whereas Peter showed wisdom in waiting for Jesus to command him to walk on the water, he subsequently failed God when he gave up believing and began to sink (Matt. 14:30–31). We should never give up on what God has told us to do.

3. *We must also spend time praying over a faith project.* We are in a spiritual battle against the powers of darkness who oppose us. It has been my experience that even with a word from God, things don't always come to pass if there has been a failure to adequately pray.

It is because Christians are being readied for the battlefield and not for a flower show that we must be prepared for trials to increase our faith. In this great war of the ages, we need to believe Him for all our spiritual, physical, and emotional needs. He wants to prove to all the powers of darkness that He can redeem us to the point of trusting in the integrity of His character no matter what!

eleven

Moving in Strategic Evangelism

In 1973, after a couple of years in Asia as a married couple, Margaret and I put roots down in Baguio City in the north of the Philippines. Nestled on a mountain slope dotted with pine trees at an altitude of five thousand feet, this bustling city then boasted four universities and one college. The city's sidewalks bulged with students to whom we felt instinctively drawn.

God's ultimate purpose in every ministry is that the lost be drawn to Christ. We didn't know how God would use our new team in evangelism, but we soon learned that winning people to Jesus doesn't just happen. It comes through purposeful effort and prayer. As we followed God's leading over the next ten years, He gave us strategies to reach the students of Baguio. Later He presented us a widening circle of opportunities that eventually encompassed much of the nation.

S oon after our arrival in Baguio, we were blessed with the visit of a New Zealand pastor. Because the house YWAM rented had a spacious living room, our team members invited many to listen to the ministry of our visiting speaker. At the first meeting, I couldn't help noticing how many college students turned up. These students had been contacted earlier by Kel Steiner and Mike Shelling, who started this YWAM center the year before. *What would happen,* I thought, *if we were to have regular meetings like this and throw it open to anyone who wanted to attend?*

Those musings developed into plans, and two weeks later, I conducted a series of meetings in which I spoke on the tough subjects of "Why do the innocent suffer?" "What about those who have never heard of Christ?" and "Is God a God of love?" These gatherings were so well attended that we announced that from then on, two meetings a week would be held in our home (affectionately called the Pink House by the locals). Given the musical and preaching abilities of a number of members on the team, it was not long before the joyful singing and faith-building sermons attracted as many as ninety youth to one meeting. Sometimes they stood at the doors or sat on the stairs because they simply had nowhere else to go!

It wasn't as if we waited for crowds to appear. We worked at it. Each morning we met to wait on the Lord, intercede, and discuss the activities of the day. Very often we ventured into nearby Burnham Park to witness to students who sat by the lake during their breaks between classes. Sometimes we visited the student dorms at night to sing, testify, and preach the gospel. At other times, new converts asked their teachers to invite us to speak in their high school or college classrooms. When possible, we'd preach at the jail. Sometimes we witnessed from house to house. We were eager to point people to Jesus, who could not only forgive their sins but also give them brand-new lives.

Vital to our presentation, both at the Pink House and at the meetings scattered around the city, were the changed lives of Filipinos on our team: Rolly, whom Christ delivered from a life of drug abuse; Fred, who had been an antigovernment agitator; Johnny, who came to Christ in our meeting in the jail; Archie, the former gang leader; and many others.

Archie's testimony was riveting. At the time one of our team members witnessed to him in the park, Archie was leading a life far from God. At times he smashed car windows and stole stereos. He and his friends had even broken into a downtown store, stolen merchandise, and then held a party with money from the sale of the stolen items. When Archie walked into one of our meetings, I was completely unaware of his background. I preached that night from Luke 19:1–10, the story of Zacchaeus the thief, who wanted to pay back what he had ripped off. The message didn't scare Archie away. As he kept in touch with our team, the truth of repentance and God's willingness to forgive him hit home. Archie came to the Lord and then began to put right what he could from his past.

Concerned that these youthful converts be *discipled* in Christ, Margaret and other team members met with them for Bible studies and to answer specific queries. In our larger public meetings, we often spoke on discipleship issues. Rolly came to see me one night after I'd taught on setting things straight with those we'd offended. We climbed the stairs together and sat on the folding wooden chairs in our small office.

"You know, brother Ross," he started earnestly, "when I came to Christ, I quit working for the post office in Manila and left without telling my boss. You see," he continued, "in my life of drugs, I borrowed three months' salary through a special post office program. Of course, I didn't tell them it was for drugs. What worries me is that they could ask my guarantor, a married man, for the money. Maybe they have already!"

I could see that God had spoken deeply to Rolly, but Rolly hadn't finished telling me all that was burdening him.

"Not only that," he continued, "I used to get my fellow employees to clock in for me on days that I was absent so I'd still get paid. I also borrowed money from them and used that money for drugs...."

I admired Rolly's openness as he poured out his story. His willingness to put things right spoke of the real conversion that had taken place. Margaret and I deeply appreciated this brother and his soft spirit.

"I tell you what, Rolly," I replied. "I'd be happy to go with you to see the postmaster general in Manila to talk about all this."

Rolly usually spoke calmly, but now his voice was pitched high with excitement and animation. "I could ask him to re-employ me without salary in exchange for all that I owe!" he said, stumbling over his words in his joyful enthusiasm.

Several days later, Rolly and I took the bus to Manila. The postmaster listened carefully to what Rolly said. He gave him back his job, saying that if he worked without pay for six weeks, the government would call it even. They owed him a few fringe benefits anyway. On the job, Rolly went to his colleagues to tell them he'd repay what he had borrowed from them. Each told him, "Never mind." They all forgave him.

"Just to see you changed is enough!" they responded. Their dismissal of his debt was a huge load off Rolly's mind. God was really helping Rolly put all of his past behind him.

God continued to use Rolly in the post office. In those days, a program within the Catholic church called the *cursillo* movement was designed to help people change their lifestyles. Those wanting to reform were invited to attend courses that were geared to help them change. Regrettably, though, many in the program fell back into their old habits. Some post office employees connected with the movement couldn't help but be impressed with Rolly's obvious transformation and wanted to know more. They invited Rolly to speak at a lunchtime post office meeting in which a hundred workers, including department heads, attended. Those in attendance sat on the edge of their chairs, enthralled with Rolly's story. What an opportunity Rolly had to describe the power of God to change lives! The proof of what Rolly was saying stood before those people. They knew him. They could see the difference. God had completely transformed his life!

A key to our evangelism efforts was those transformed lives. So also were the friendships between those who'd come to Christ and their classmates. Because relational ties are extremely strong in the Philippines, the new converts naturally brought their friends to our meetings in the Pink House, which had now become a student center. The newcomers also would often give their lives to Christ.

In turn, these joyous young people paved the way for us to preach, sing, and act out our skits in different parts of the city. Or they would invite us to their hometowns miles away. We gladly accepted. Most memorable was the time team members were invited to the municipality of Mayoyao, which then could be accessed only through a trail that snaked through the valleys and over the mountains. The trip took two days by buses that ground away in low gear near steep cliffs overlooking green valleys far below. As team members preached and testified, God's Spirit moved with such conviction that villagers returned stolen items, such as live chickens they'd snatched!

In addition, our teams journeyed all over the Philippines, even to Mindanao in the far south, preaching discipleship themes in churches and youth groups, and preaching the gospel in schools. Many came to Christ. We learned to make use of the evangelism opportunities on the way, especially on the inter-island ferries. We usually traveled third class, and in these compartments, long lines of stretcherlike cots were butted up against each other. Since passengers had little to do, we would sing to them and witness for Christ.

On one twenty-four-hour sailing to the island of Samar, our team of six went throughout the ship singing gospel choruses to the accompaniment of Fred's guitar. The passengers listened attentively to us as we testified and preached in either English, Tagalog, or the language of Samar. Finally, a crew member invited us to the captain's bridge with its spectacular view of the blue ocean in all directions. For one full hour, the six of us sang, testified, and preached over the loudspeaker system that reached into every quarter of the ship!

From broadcasting to that entire ship, we eventually were invited to broadcast our testimonies and messages by radio in a number of cities as we traveled the Philippines over the years. But we didn't always wait to be invited to preach. If we sensed an opening was right, we took it, just as the apostle Paul exhorted us with respect to nonbelievers, "[M]ake the most of every opportunity" (Col. 4:5).

One experience was particularly memorable. After a long bus ride to Manila one day, Paul Roberts and I stood at the curb in a congested part of town known for drug use. We'd been trying to hail a taxi for a minute or two when I sensed something was wrong. I looked down to check on our bags.

"Paul, where's *your* bag?" I asked when I couldn't see it. In that short space of time, it had completely vanished!

In response, Paul walked up and down the street with his hands raised, passionately asking people if they'd seen his bag. No one said a word. People didn't know or didn't want to know what had happened to the bag. Meanwhile, the sight of Paul, a foreigner with long red hair swirling in the breeze and hands raised, attracted a curious gathering. People appeared from everywhere! I couldn't help feeling this was too good an opportunity to pass up. After all, we were missionaries called to share the gospel of Christ. *That bag has been stolen. We'll never see it again,* I thought. But we could redeem this situation a little.

"Paul," I said, lowering my voice while looking at the crowd that thronged around us four or five deep, "why don't we preach? Would you be willing to give your testimony?" Paul nodded, although somewhat hesitantly.

"Excuse me, everybody!" I said, lifting my hands to grasp their attention. "We are two young missionaries who have just arrived by bus from Baguio. We are in your country telling people about Jesus Christ, who wants to give you a new life." I continued to preach for a few more minutes and then introduced Paul.

"With me is a young man from Colorado who used to take drugs. But by the power of God, he has been radically *changed.* That is what happens when you give your life to Christ. What God has done for others, He can do for you. If you turn from all that you know is wrong and give your life to Him, He'll change you. My friend Paul is now going to tell you what happened to him."

I motioned to Paul to begin.

"Yes, folks…it's true. Before I gave my life to Jesus, I took many drugs," Paul started rather falteringly. He described his past life and the difference Jesus had made. I could tell, though, that he was laboring under the weight of the loss of his bag.

Even so, I was surprised when he suddenly raised both arms again and blurted out, "Has anybody seen my bag?"

Paul's actions effectively stopped our street meeting, although I continued to talk to interested people who still milled around. When most had dispersed, a couple of shady-looking characters called us over to a back wall.

"Tell us where you are staying," one of them said, not looking me in the eye. "We'll see what we can do about the bag."

We gave them our address, but I held out no hope of ever seeing Paul's bag again. We finally piled into a taxi and headed downtown. As we traveled, Paul told me he was particularly disappointed that he had lost his big Bible. He wasn't so worried about his other belongings. "Just to get that Bible back would be wonderful!"

No one was more surprised than I two hours later. After doing business downtown, we reached our little YWAM Manila apartment to find Paul's bag waiting for us!

Moving in Strategic Evangelism

Steve Tackett, director of YWAM Nashville, once told me, "Becoming born again was such an awesome experience and so different from my churchgoing background that my response was, 'More people ought to know about this.'"

This response is precisely the reaction Jesus intended all Christians to have. Jesus expected His disciples to travel the world "gossiping the gospel" in a positive, life-giving way. Exactly how we go about that will depend largely on our personalities, what opportunities exist, and the prevailing culture. In most of Roman Catholic Philippines, it was comparatively easy to spread the Word of God. Not all cultures, however, will allow that freedom. In closed countries, more discreet means need to be used. Wherever we spread the gospel, however, certain principles are universal.

1. *A relationship exists between sowing and reaping.* Notice the sowing that took place all over Baguio City and the subsequent reaping. The early Church gathered in a large harvest of new believers, who, we know "went out and preached everywhere." (Mark 16:20). Even persecution did not stop them: "Those who had been scattered preached the word wherever they went" (Acts 8:4).

2. *We are to promote God's character when we evangelize.* While He was on earth, Jesus represented to man what God the Father is like. No wonder the crowds "were amazed at the gracious words that came from his lips" (Luke 4:22). The temple guards sent to arrest Jesus reported back to the Pharisees empty-handed, saying, "No one ever spoke the way this man does" (John 7:46).

Jesus said, "But I, when I am lifted up…will draw all men to myself" (John 12:32). Specifically, He meant being lifted up on the Cross. Powerfully implied is the fact that it's the character of God (represented by Jesus's self-denial on the Cross for our sins) that we are to share when we witness for Christ. The Bible tells us it is the goodness of God that leads us to repentance (Rom. 2:4). That is why we must always evangelize in a friendly manner. God wants us to woo people to Him, not beat them into submission.*

3. *Real repentance is necessary for true conversion.* Consider the story of Jesus and Zacchaeus. While it is true that Jesus loved Zacchaeus while he was perched in the tree, Zacchaeus

---

* For further explanation of this and other points on evangelism, see *We Cannot But Tell: A Practical Guide to Heart to Heart Evangelism* by Ross Tooley (YWAM Publishing, 1993).

wasn't declared saved until he demonstrated his repentance (Luke 19:5–9).

We all know that God's love is unconditional, for He loves the just and the unjust (Matt. 5:44–45), but His salvation is another matter. It is very conditional. We have to truly repent and trust the work on Christ's Cross to receive it (Acts 17:30–31; John 1:12). In the Philippines, we were blessed to see some outstanding conversions as we preached true repentance—conversions we would not have otherwise seen. However, for the preaching of repentance to be effective, the sinner needs to be overwhelmed by the loving character of God (Rom. 2:4).

Part of repentance is being reconciled with those we have hurt—whether we inflicted the pain by means of material loss or by wounding through a broken relationship. When in real humility we go back to those we've hurt and put things right (e.g., make restitution), we demonstrate the character of God. Many are attracted to Christ as a result.

Stephen Arterburn, founder and president of New Life Treatment Centers in California, formerly worked for a clothing store and wrongfully took clothes home on a regular basis. After he came to Christ, he wanted to put his misdeed right. Although he figured the merchandise he stole came to one thousand dollars, he sent a check for well over that amount to his former manager. He fully expected to do jail time. The manager was so impressed with Steve's obviously changed life that he didn't press charges. Not only that, he decided to follow Christ as well!

A divorced man came to a Billy Graham meeting with the woman who had been the reason for his marriage breakup. The evangelist's message on family convicted this man deeply. During the call for people to receive Christ, the divorced man looked up to see his former wife respond. Broken before God, he left his seat to stand beside the one he had betrayed, not only to give his life to God but also to be reconciled with his wife.

When people are really repentant, the justice of God as well as the love of God will be seen. But just a note of caution. When it comes to sexual sin, great wisdom has to be exercised if you want to apologize to a former sexual partner. Great damage can result if your former partner's spouse is not aware of your past liaison and now, without warning, finds out. Even if your former partner is still single, there are hidden pitfalls. I strongly suggest you pray with a pastor or trusted spiritual leader before you act.

4. *Intercession is a key.* In the Philippines, we interceded before every witnessing session or meeting in a classroom or dorm. God has always intended prayer to be an integral part of evangelism. One has only to look at the book of Acts to see how powerfully the early Church interceded and how correspondingly effective they were in evangelism. The apostles declared, "[We] will give our attention to prayer and the ministry of the word" (Acts 6:4). If we want to see "Book of Acts" results, we must use "Book of Acts" principles. The emphasis the early Church placed on prayer, waiting on God, and intercession is clearly seen in Acts 1:14; 4:29; 12:5; Ephesians 6:18–20; and Colossians 4:2–4, 12.

5. *God has promised to provide materially for those who put his kingdom first.* The message of the gospel is so important that God promises to supply our needs as we seek first His kingdom (Matt. 6:33). I don't believe we would have retrieved Paul's bag if I'd not preached that day. Not that I preached to get it back. Nor did I preach to try to make anyone feel guilty for stealing the bag. My preaching was done out of love for God and the lost. If we're concerned about the kingdom of God, He will worry about our material needs, even our bags!

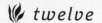 *twelve*

Being Faithful in Little Things

It may or may not come as a surprise to you, but how we use material possessions determines our level of God-given spiritual authority. Jesus taught, "[I]f you have not been trustworthy in handling worldly wealth, who will trust you with true riches?" (Luke 16:11). Stewardship of material items is therefore like an apprenticeship. The "true riches," of course, include getting to know God better, hearing His voice more clearly, and being a channel for His power through our God-given talents.

During our years of service in Baguio City, God gave me graphic lessons on this subject that brought things into focus for me. He made very clear to me the connection between how we handle what He has already given us and our effectiveness in our ministry.

*O*ne of my coworkers in Baguio was a congenial young man named Graeme Jones, who helped me lead the YWAM center. In 1976, Graeme and his wife were about to leave for a few months of further training at our Pacific headquarters in Kona, Hawaii. Before they said good-bye, Graeme graciously handed me the keys to their thirteen-seater all-purpose Ford jeepney. As our YWAM center had no vehicle of its own, the loan of this sky-blue vehicle was a great blessing.

Several months later, we traveled to the United States to attend a worldwide Youth With A Mission staff conference. When we returned six weeks later, I could not help noticing the run-down state of the jeepney we'd borrowed. I'd obviously failed to pass on to my coworkers a value I had learned in childhood: Always take care of what you have borrowed. The once neat-looking jeepney appeared unkempt and dirty. A front headlight bulb had blown, and the plastic windows were torn. I was particularly disappointed because Graeme wanted to sell the vehicle to pay for the training in Hawaii. *We're going to have to do something about this,* I thought.

A message given at a Sunday morning church service by Dr. Grover Tyner, the president of the Philippine Baptist Theological Seminary in Baguio, jolted me into immediate action. I sat up in my seat when Dr. Tyner preached about stewardship from Luke 16:10–12. I took particular note of verse 12: "And if you have not been trustworthy with someone else's property, who will give you property of your own?" I'd never noticed that link before. Of course! If our base wanted to own a vehicle, we'd need to be careful with the one we had borrowed.

At our student center that very afternoon, I preached from the same passage of Scripture, saying, "If we don't get that vehicle into the condition it was in before we received it, God will not give us our own vehicle. In fact, we should return things we borrow in even better condition than when we received them!"

And so we set to work until the vehicle looked better than before the Joneses had left. About a month later, I could hardly believe my eyes as I held a check for four thousand dollars from YWAM Canada. For us in YWAM in the Philippines, the size of the gift was astronomical and totally unheard of! When I read the accompanying letter from Uli Kortch, the YWAM Canadian director, my heart skipped a beat.

"The check is for the purchase of vehicles for your center." What I found even more intriguing was Uli's handwritten note at the bottom of the typed page. "We've had this money for several months," it read, "but it's only now that we have felt led to send it. Could you give us some understanding about this?"

Could I? *Could I ever!* I thrilled at God's wisdom to restrain Uli from sending the money until we had learned our lesson. As disciples, we are to always thirst to know God's ways (Psa. 103:7). This was one of them. God wants us to treat other people's property with care. Then He'll entrust us with our own.

We immediately sent a check for two thousand dollars to Graeme as complete payment for the Ford. He at first thought it was some sort of joke. He *knew* we wouldn't have that sort of money. Well, we surprised him! With the rest we bought a four-wheel-drive Chevrolet Blazer to negotiate the rough mountain roads north of Baguio that led to such isolated places as Mayoyao.

Faithfulness with *borrowed* things was only one part of Jesus' message on stewardship (Luke 16:10–12). Another part of His sermon relates to faithfulness in *little* things, and we were about to learn that the principle didn't apply just to financial matters. It would work in ministry issues, too. This lesson actually started earlier, but it would be a while before we would see it more clearly.

Two years before, we'd shown the college students at our center a 16-mm movie about the one thousand YWAMers who had sung and witnessed on the streets of Munich during the 1972 Olympic Games. We borrowed a projector and screened the film on an old bedsheet we'd strung up for the occasion.

Spurred on by the excitement generated by this showing, we showed the movie around the city. In schools and churches, or even in the street, crowds of people stood to watch. A year later, we received another film and did the rounds once more. Each showing further confirmed to us the drawing power of a movie in the Philippines. When we were given a brand-new projector in 1976 (God had noticed we had been faithfully using a borrowed one around town), we loaded up all the equipment and team members in the blue jeepney and once more showed the very same movie around the city!

Later, I felt impressed to take this same film to a television station in Manila that agreed to show it free of charge. When the leader of a Manila library of sixty Christian movies heard what we'd done, he told me, "Hey, Ross, you can use any of our films to show on television."

I was ecstatic! Whenever I was in Manila after that, I stopped by whenever I could to watch one of his movies. I was particularly on the lookout for those that would speak to secular audiences. After two months of watching these films and approaching television stations, we were delighted when a station called with the question, "What movies do you have that we could show during the coming Easter season?"

One film was called *The Rapture*. Set in the format of a newscast, the film depicts one interpretation of what might be seen on the evening news in the United States just after Christ's return. Channel 7 showed it during prime time the night before Easter Sunday 1977, with literally millions of Filipinos tuned in to watch it. Staff at the TV studio reported that it generated the biggest response to a movie they'd ever had!

Even without the hindsight of today, I could see then what was happening. As we'd been faithful with what Jesus called in Luke 16:10 "very little" (one short movie), God had increased the scope of our ministry thousands of times over! What we didn't foresee was how God would expand the vision. Later that year, I was previewing a Billy Graham movie in Manila when God surprised me with a totally unexpected thought. *The movie you are watching needs to be shown in theaters throughout the country!*

It took a lot of planning, but four months later, we ran *Two a Penny* using two 16-mm projectors in a small Baguio theater for four days to almost five thousand people. Even then we still couldn't see what lay ahead.

Eventually our teams crisscrossed the archipelago promoting several standard 35-mm Christian films that filled huge screens in public theaters—often to standing-room-only crowds. Hundreds of thousands from northern Luzon to southern Mindanao watched these Christian movies. We passed out literature we had specially written, spoke in high school classes and civic clubs, and were interviewed on radio and television throughout the Philippines. Just in the area of our movie ministry alone, we found ourselves with a nationwide ministry!

It all started with one 16-mm film, a borrowed projector, and an old bedsheet!* Doing what we could with something little had allowed God to anoint our team for even bigger things. This is exactly what Jesus taught us in Luke 16:10.

---

* See *Adventures in Naked Faith* by Ross Tooley (YWAM Publishing, 1996) for a fuller account of this very productive time in our ministry.

Being Faithful in Little Things

God has reasons for sending His blessing and reasons for withholding it. As Loren Cunningham once said, "God does not want to multiply a mess." The following principles that Jesus stressed in Luke 16:10–12 are just as important today as they have ever been.

1. *Faithfulness in little things determines whether or not more important things will follow.* Jesus preached, "Whoever can be trusted with very little can also be trusted with much, and whoever is dishonest with very little will also be dishonest with much" (verse 10).

Sometimes we excuse ourselves for failing to fulfill a commitment or expectation by saying, "It was just a little thing!" That is not a reason God honors. Jesus indicated that we'll treat the big situations with the same attitude we demonstrate in the smaller items. How we regard an overdue library book, for example, could be the same way we'd deal with a spiritual engagement. Worse, it might reflect how we'd deal with a hurting individual or someone who needs salvation.

2. *Faithfulness with borrowed things determines whether or not we will eventually get our own possessions.* Jesus said, "And if you have not been trustworthy with someone else's property, who will give you property of your own?" (verse 12). As parents, we would, for example, find it difficult to give our children their own sporting goods when they have left our equipment out in the rain or treated it in some other careless manner. Our children obviously haven't yet proved themselves trustworthy in this regard.

3. *Faithfulness with material things determines our ability to handle spiritual authority.* Jesus stated, " So if you have not been trustworthy in handling worldly wealth, who will trust you with true riches?" (verse 11).

How does God decide we are ready to lead, teach, or counsel others or exercise our other God-given gifts? One way is through observing the use of our material possessions. While the abuse of material things is regrettable, it is not as serious as the abuse of spiritual power. That is why God employs the "apprenticeship" method of the use of our material articles before He gives us spiritual authority. The misuse of spiritual authority—whether by leading, counseling, or preaching—can do devastating damage. Many who have come out from a controlling or oppressive religious environment say that it has taken them years to recover. Ultimately, damage done by spiritual leadership to someone's soul can be more devastating than damage done to the body.

Faithfulness is a Christian virtue because it is so much a part of God's character. Suppose God forgot to cause the sun to shine or the rain to fall? Or failed to monitor the mix of oxygen and nitrogen in the air? In 2 Timothy 2:2, Paul instructed his protégé Timothy to pass on to *faithful* men the teachings of the early Church. God would far rather train disciples of average intelligence He can trust than brilliantly talented ones He can't depend on.

Our faithfulness in little things is like a barometer. God tests and proves us to be sure we are *faithful* before He gives us additional spiritual authority. These testings are a necessary part of a Christian's journey to spiritual maturity.

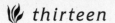 *thirteen*

Learning the Power
of Intercession

We Christians know it's right to pray. Jesus and spiritual heroes throughout the ages have set that example for us. We know that there's never been a man or woman of God who has not been a person of prayer and intercession. We're convinced that we come closer to God and receive guidance through prayer. The question we all ask, however, either consciously or unconsciously, is, What good does it do beyond that? Isn't it true that whatever will be, will be?

Over the years of my ministry, I've received many encouragements that intercessory prayer does makes a huge difference, that through this discipline, things happen that wouldn't otherwise occur. One striking example for me occurred the day that God led me and my partners in ministry to intercede intensely for an impossible situation in Manila. Afterward, it was as if the Red Sea had opened up right before our eyes.

*I*n 1978, after five years in Baguio, Margaret and I felt very much at home. We loved what God was doing and enjoyed the fellowship of the students whom God had touched. We were excited when Filipino staff members went on missions throughout the nation to testify, preach, or promote Christian movies. But God had further things in store for them.

The M/V *Logos*, a ship owned by Operation Mobilization (OM), was in Manila that year as part of an evangelism and book-selling tour. We always appreciated fellowship with OM's workers when the ship docked in a Philippine port. Graeme Jones and I had even lectured on board when the ship visited Saigon before the fall of South Vietnam. We had watched in amazement as long, zigzagging lines of Vietnamese inched toward the ship to buy Christian literature. It was a joy to see the international OM workers sent out in teams to preach whenever they could in schools or churches. OM has always desired that its teams be a multicultural mix, and the ship's workers were no exception to this rule.

While the ship was in Manila, Margaret and I met David Hicks, the ship's director. In one of our conversations, David asked if Filipinos in our group could travel and minister with them on board the M/V *Logos*. My heart quickened at the idea of their pitching in and ministering in Japan, Korea, and Taiwan, the next ports of call. For years I'd wanted our Filipino brethren to minister in the more needy Buddhist areas of Asia, but given the Philippines' economy, the cost of travel was a deterrent. Even the tax levied on an air ticket was exorbitant.

This new opportunity, however, meant no airfare and no travel tax! Yet as David spoke, reality struck home. "They'd have to get their passports before we leave our tour of the Philippines next month," he added.

In many countries, that would be a simple matter. But under the martial law rule of then president Ferdinand Marcos, it presented a big obstacle. In addition to having the customary birth certificate, Filipinos needed clearances from local police and the National Bureau of Investigation. They had to line up for hours at crowded government agencies and pay all sorts of fees. Even that didn't guarantee a passport. Under martial law, the authorities scrutinized every applicant. They denied passports to those whose reasons for international travel were considered unnecessary. Even for those with valid reasons, the process was painfully slow, necessitating time-consuming follow-up visits to a number of government agencies.

Nevertheless, I approached Filipino staff members with the idea. After a lot of prayer and consideration of practical matters, it emerged that the three most likely to travel would be Rey Yap, Sammy Tenizo, and Fred Sanchez. Everything proved a challenge: the poor telecommunications system in those days, the slowness of the mail, and the lethargy of government red tape. It didn't seem to matter that Sammy had previously had a passport, now expired.

All this proved nerve-wracking. While the bureaucratic process dragged on, the fixed departure date crept ominously closer. With only two weeks to go, the three young men left Baguio to work on board the *Logos* while it was docked in Manila. They worked hard and long, moving books around the ship or directing the flow of visitors on board. The passport office was so close to the port that they regularly checked up on their papers. From time to time they sent a report to us in

Baguio, which fueled our intercession for them. The whole affair proved an emotional roller-coaster ride both for them and for us as we prayed. Despite all their multiplied efforts, nothing happened. The day before departure, not even one passport had been issued!

Team member Bob Grierson, a bearded young man with a soft heart, joined me as I traveled by bus to Manila to pray and offer encouragement. When we arrived that night, we found the atmosphere subdued. The month of working on their papers had been hard work. One of the trio was openly pessimistic.

"It's hopeless. We'll never make it now!"

"You know, guys," I said in the brightest spirit I could muster, "I still believe it's God's will for you to go. The ship doesn't sail until 2 P.M. tomorrow. That means there's still time for those passports to be issued."

We prayed. But in the somber mood that prevailed, we all realized the odds were stacked against us.

Early the next morning, Fred and Rey set off on a crowded jeepney for the passport section of the Department of Foreign Affairs. The rest of us headed with the luggage through Manila's noisy, bumper-to-bumper traffic to the ship. Once on board, Sammy returned to his work in the hold. Bob and I stationed ourselves on steps near the bow of the ship in semiprivacy. This would be our "prayer room."

Known for his reliability, Fred dutifully called in hourly reports. The first account was not promising. Nor was the second one.

"It's bedlam down here as people jostle for position," he told me over the phone. I knew the no-frills office. The noise of the crowd would reverberate around the drab cement floor and walls. The challenge would be to get to the clerks standing behind solid iron grills. There would be no lining up, and only those who managed to poke their papers through the grill would get attended to. In this kind of atmosphere, it was easy to be overlooked.

"Keep on trying," I encouraged Fred in an endeavor to keep his spirits up. "We're really praying for you!"

I was particularly mystified as to why Sammy's passport hadn't been released. Since Sammy had previously traveled to Hawaii for a training course, I figured at the very least they would issue a new passport for him. But I didn't know about the prevalence of fake passports, which made getting a renewal just as difficult as getting a new one.

By this time, Bob and I had prayed for an hour or two, but after the second negative report, we switched into battle mode. The ship would sail in just a few hours! We addressed the powers of darkness and told them they had no authority in this matter. We reminded them that their eternal destination was set. We persistently kept up the prayer vigil, with Bob and me praying back and forth and occasionally at the same time. We prayed the Word of God back to heaven as Moses had done when he reminded the Lord of His promises (Ex. 32:13). I had found that kind of prayer helpful over the years. We reminded the Lord that His gospel was to go into all the world (Matt. 24:14) and that the object of our intercession was for His glory.

By 11 A.M. there was no change. Shortly after that, one of the ship's officials found me and asked about the status of the passports. I hesitantly replied, "We don't have any yet."

"Well, it looks like they won't be able to sail with us," he said, lowering his voice. "We have to submit all passports to the immigration authorities soon so the ship can be cleared for departure."

"Could we give it a little extra time?" I pleaded. "Two of the boys are right now at the Department of Foreign Affairs. There's still time for God to release those passports."

The official looked at me dubiously but said nothing. I could understand what was probably going through his mind. *If a month wasn't long enough, what good would another hour do?*

Back at our position on the steps, Bob and I again prayed fervently. It made no difference to us that we could be heard by others. We were convinced that the trio should sail at 2 P.M. We also knew that our only recourse was intercession. I was so glad for Bob's friendship and devotion to prayer. This prayer vigil would have been extremely difficult without him.

Around 11:30 A.M., Fred called excitedly. "They said they'll issue my passport!"

"Great!" I almost shouted into the phone. "But what about the others?"

"As soon as I got mine, Rey stepped up to the counter through the throng and said, 'What about me?'"

I grinned. A doctor's son, Rey was neither pushy nor vocal. But I could picture him, faced with being left behind, politely muscling his way to the front, excusing himself as he went.

"So what did they say?"

"They told him, 'No, you won't get yours!'" Then Fred added, "But Rey is still standing by!"

"Good!" I replied. "Tell him to hang in there. We'll continue to intercede. What about Sammy's passport?"

"Still nothing! But I keep asking about it. We'll just keep waiting. But, brother Ross, it's really crowded and noisy down here!"

I was still mystified that Sammy's passport had not been granted. Losing no time, I asked someone to take the news to Sammy in the hold and excitedly filled Bob in. Inspired by the progress report, we enthusiastically entered into even more spirited, vocal prayer. We fervently rebuked the powers of darkness and called on God to intervene. It wasn't like being in a war. It *was* war! *Spiritual war!*

Half an hour later, Fred called again.

"Rey's got his passport!"

"Great! But what about Sammy's?" I asked, my voice going up an octave.

"It's still not released."

"You'll need to be here at 1 P.M. at the latest," I insisted. I figured that with the release of two passports, the ship's crew and the immigration authorities would give us more time.

Bob and I continued the vigil and kept our prayers ascending. We kept reminding the Lord that we believed it was His will that these boys promote the work of the gospel via the M/V *Logos*. We kept rebuking the powers of darkness that would deny Sammy his passport.

Finally, a half hour later, Fred called with the news. "Sammy's passport will be issued!"

The battle was still not over, however. Fred's real name was Rudolfo, and that was proving to be a sticky point. Fred would have to wait until an official arrived to sign his application. If the official didn't sign before the 1 P.M. closing time, Fred would be left behind. We continued to pray. Finally, Fred's passport was released right at 1 P.M., and Fred rushed to the ship. When he appeared, I was so excited I could hardly keep my feet on the ground!

The M/V *Logos* weighed anchor and began its maneuvers to leave port. Bob and I and the others from Baguio who had been volunteers on board watched with great thankfulness to God, especially as we saw Sammy, Rey, and Fred smiling and waving from the deck of the ship!

Postscript

Over the next four months, the boys worked long hours on board the ship in the ports of Okinawa and Yokohama (Japan), Pusan and Inchon (Korea), and Keelung and Kaohsiung

(Taiwan). Sammy trusted God for the finances to leave the ship in Japan to attend a large month-long evangelistic outreach in Argentina during the 1978 World Cup soccer games. He returned to Baguio replete with stories of how God had provided for his airfare both to and from Buenos Aires. A local Baguio newspaper published a report of Sammy's time abroad, which launched me into writing a Christian column each week for that newspaper. Rey and Fred had their own stories to tell when they finally returned.

Learning the Power of Intercession

A number of guidelines about the subject of intercession arise from this story.

1. *Stick to the prayer subject.* Answers to prayer often don't come with one-liners. Many times, God asks us to continue in intercession until He lifts the burden. Elijah's praying seven times on Mount Carmel until the rain fell is but one illustration (1 Kings 18:43–45). Another is the example of the apostle Paul's friend Epaphras, who was "always *wrestling* in prayer" for the Colossian church, that they may "stand firm in all the will of God" (Col. 4:12, emphasis added).

If we stay on the subject, God will reveal just how He wants us to pray. Sometimes He'll tell us what the enemy is trying to do and how we are to combat him. It is my experience that the devil gets nervous when Christians evangelize, go on mission trips, or seek to influence today's media. Little wonder that we are instructed to be alert in these areas (1 Peter 5:8–9) and to *devote* ourselves to prayer, being watchful (Col. 4:2).

2. *Companionship can be vital.* Without Bob, I would not have sustained the fervency of prayer that was needed in the story just related. While we are all called to pray alone, there is

real value in praying with someone committed to the same goal (Deut. 32:30).

When you are an extrovert like me, having a partner is critical. For years I wondered why I interceded longer and more fervently with a friend than I did by myself. Why didn't I have the same tenacity alone? Then I discovered that extroverts need to put things into words much more than others. Often it's when I articulate something that it makes more sense or, in some cases, I realize the incorrectness of what I'm thinking! I can therefore pray more meaningfully when I pray aloud. While introverts are capable of interceding for long hours by themselves, I personally find that difficult.

3. *Pray back the Word of God.* In Exodus 32:13–14, God was about to destroy the nation of Israel, but Moses reminded God of His promise and prayed, "Remember your servants Abraham, Isaac and Israel, to whom you swore by your own self: 'I will make your descendants as numerous as the stars in the sky and I will give your descendants all this land I promised them, and it will be their inheritance forever.'" Coming at the end of a powerful time of prayer, this spiritual activity of reminding God of His promises had an immediate impact. "Then the LORD relented and did not bring on his people the disaster he had threatened" (verse 14).

4. *Intercession moves God's hand.* I've observed that God often requires our intercession before He makes a move. Such a stance is substantiated in the Scriptures, where we're told in Psalm 106:23 that if Moses had not interceded for the people of Israel (in the episode just referred to), God would have destroyed them.

In Isaiah 38, we read a revealing incident when God told Hezekiah he was about to die. Not submitting to fatalism, however, the righteous king wept and prayed. God hearkened to

Hezekiah and granted him another fifteen years. Remarkable to the story is this: Had Hezekiah not been granted those extra years, Judah would never have seen King Josiah, one of the most righteous kings ever. It was under Josiah's righteous reign that many far-reaching reforms were effected (2 Chron. 34:1–35:19).

5. *Resist the devil.* We must deal firmly with Satan, for he constantly interferes when he has no authority to. Because of Jesus' work on the Cross, the devil has no right to oppose us, yet many times he does. He is called a usurper (someone who acts without authority). That's why resisting him is so important. Obviously, we have to be in right standing with the Lord to do this. James says, *"Submit yourselves, then, to God. Resist the devil, and he will flee from you"* (James 4:7, emphasis added).

6. *Our motives must be pure.* I once prayed that many would attend a meeting where I was going to speak. I was shocked when God revealed my motive for the prayer. It wasn't that God would be glorified. My real reason for the prayer was that I wanted the meeting to enhance my image. I had to repent for wanting God to simply fulfill my own ends. Incidents like this make me realize we need to regularly examine our motives for praying "for Jesus' sake." The use of those three words is supposed to mean that only Jesus will get the benefit and the glory if the prayer is answered.

7. *Faith is the key.* Someone once said, "God hears our prayers but answers our faith." God loves bold prayers because we know something is His will and because we believe in His character. He really wants us to take Him at His Word. We are more likely to receive what we believe for than what we doubt for. Without faith, it is impossible to please Him (Heb. 11:6). It is important to worship God for who He is and praise Him for His mighty deeds *before* He answers, for that proves our faith. It reveals that we believe that God is bigger than our present

circumstances, even if they mean being at the mercy of the martial law government of President Marcos!

Whether we like it or not, a war rages between the powers of darkness and the powers of righteousness. But God has ordained that through intercession the body of Christ should drive back those forces that oppose God's will being done on earth—just as Israel prevailed when Moses' hands were lifted up.

fourteen

Receiving Revelation

One exciting ingredient of intense, Spirit-led prayer is the revelation God often gives. God wants to share His thoughts with those who stay persistently in His presence. He often shows things to those who consistently pray for the subject God has laid on their hearts.

During the political chaos that followed the Philippine elections in the 1980s, a group of us began to fiercely intercede for the nation over a period of time. As we began, we knew, of course, that God reveals things as His people pray. But we could never have known what God had in mind to share with us at that time.

With the revelation came responsibility—and a few interesting assignments.

N o matter what I put my mind to, I couldn't shake the thought: *Contact the leader of the Catholic charismatic group at Malacanang, the presidential palace. Offer the team and their drama for the meeting tomorrow.*

Frankly, I was getting tired of it. I felt embarrassed to present the proposal at such short notice. I told myself, *It's already Thursday, and the group meets at lunchtime Friday!*

It was 1982, and I'd been in Manila working with YWAM's Far East Evangelistic Team (FEET) from Hong Kong, arranging many meetings for them. At the center of FEET's program that year was a forty-five-minute mime presentation called *Tribute.* Team members performed in white tuxedos while stirring background music with pieces from *The Young Messiah* kept toes tapping and audiences captivated. It was easy to share Christ after each performance.

These meetings were most appropriate for the new spiritual climate in the Philippines. Over recent years, a phenomenon had occurred in predominantly Catholic Manila, where scores of charismatic meetings (both Catholic and Protestant) had mushroomed all over the metropolis. Often led by laypeople, these groups met at places of work—in private businesses like IBM or in government offices like the Bureau of Immigration—rather than houses of worship. For those of us who'd witnessed for Christ in the Philippines for years, this turn of events was nearly unbelievable. I had been privileged to speak at many of these gatherings, and it thrilled me to see the hunger people had for the Lord.

Headquarters for our operation was a downtown Manila church, where we all slept on air mattresses thrown over the rough cement floor. As I strung up my mosquito net between four wooden chairs placed in the middle of the sanctuary floor that night, the nagging thought persisted. *You really should contact the group at the president's palace!* When I slid under the mosquito net, I finally quieted my conscience by resolving to "pray about the thought in the morning."

The traffic noise outside the church ensured that I was awake around 5:30 the next morning. Still under the mosquito net, I riffled through the pages of my Bible to start my quiet time with the Lord. Reaching my place, I began to read Jeremiah 22. My heart soon missed a beat as I stared at the instructions originally intended for the prophet Jeremiah. The instructions from God suddenly lit up as if they were meant for me. Or was I imagining things? I had not come to my reading expecting anything like this. But remembering the impression I'd battled the day before, my eyes stayed glued to the words, "This is what the LORD says: 'Go down to the palace…and proclaim this message there…'" (Jer. 22:1).

Could this be God? Am I really to take the team to Malacanang palace? Or am I off the wall?

As I read on, I noticed that the conditions of corruption and chaos in Jeremiah's day paralleled those of the Philippines. After prayer, I decided I was to approach Matt Rawlins, the cordial young leader of FEET. As we all stood around a breakfast of fresh *pan de sal* (bread), coffee, and bananas, I told Matt what was on my heart.

Several hours later, after much prayer and consultation with the team, Matt gave me the go-ahead to contact Malacanang. "If they say we can come at this late stage, we'll do the performance." Excited, I left to find a telephone, as the church had none of its own. I had to use the phone of a roadside store on a noisy street to call the palace of the president of the Philippines!

I dialed the numbers on the old black phone and concentrated hard to hear above the roar of the traffic that hurtled past me. I glanced quickly at my watch. *Nine o'clock!* What a time to call. The meeting would start at noon! Feeling embarrassed, I could see I was still learning the old lesson. Pride and obeying God don't go together. To cope with my awkwardness, I reminded myself it was more important to follow the leading of the Lord. Just then my contact answered the phone, and I apologized immediately for the lateness of the request.

"Oh, that's okay," the voice at the other end said. "We would be delighted to have your drama team come!" We chatted for a few minutes, and then I ended the conversation. As I hung up, I let out a sigh of relief.

As the team prepared for the coming engagement, I mused on Jeremiah 22. Verse 3 was particularly relevant to the administration of President Marcos: "Do what is just and right. Rescue from the hand of his oppressor the one who has been robbed. Do no wrong…in this place."

A few hours later, FEET gave its rousing performance in a high-ceilinged meeting room of the palace that had been the governor's mansion during Spanish colonial days. Afterward I stood behind the podium and looked out at the audience that had gathered. I described the moral conditions of Jeremiah's day and the warning the prophet gave to the nation of Judah. Then I zeroed in on the present.

"God still judges nations by how they respond morally to His code," I warned. As diplomatically as I could, I continued. "Without righteousness, there will not be a peaceful transition to a new administration in this country." I quoted from Jeremiah 22:5: "But if you do not obey these commands, declares the LORD…*this palace will become a ruin*" (emphasis added).

Margaret and I and our three boys—Mark, ten; Stuart, seven; and Warren, four—later moved to Hawaii, and these events were largely forgotten over the next few years. At the University of the Nations campus on the Kona coast, I attended several courses. Then at the beginning of 1986, I traveled to Tyler, Texas, to attend an author's training school. In intercession times, we often prayed for the elections in the Philippines in which Marcos was running against the lowly widow of slain Senator Begnino Aquino. Knowing that Mrs. Aquino's late husband, had he not been assassinated, would have been a shoo-in for president, crowds flocked to her rallies.

After polling day, suspicions were raised worldwide that Marcos was deliberately slowing down the vote counting to tamper with the results. An unofficial tally put Mrs. Corazon Aquino comfortably ahead, yet Marcos was always "just winning" in the slow returns released by the government.

Several of us at the writers' school had worked in the Philippines, which motivated us to pray passionately for justice to prevail. The intensity of our concern rose with every news bulletin, especially when the secretary of defense and the armed forces chief of staff openly broke with the government. Declaring that Marcos had not won the election, they barricaded themselves in at a city army base on a wide boulevard called Epifanio de los Santos Avenue. Later, the Roman Catholic cardinal of Manila called on the masses to surround the defectors as human shields. As many as a million people poured onto the boulevard and neighboring streets as a result.

Tension mounted when Marcos ordered tanks into the area. Anxiety rose even higher when part of the air force sided with the rebels. Open fighting broke out in some streets. I couldn't believe what was happening in the land I loved!

At the pinnacle of the tensions, our concern was so strong that the school gathered in one group one afternoon to pray for an extended period. I fervently prayed for God to intervene. My concern was such that I told God He could miraculously translate me to Manila in the same way Philip was whisked away in the Bible (Acts 8:39–40). I was so burdened, I'd be prepared to stand in front of the tanks as I had heard Filipinos were doing. I meant every word I prayed.

I was still burdened at bedtime. What would happen in the Philippines? Would Marcos open fire on the million or so citizens who had gathered around Camp Crame where the secretary of defense and armed forces chief of staff were barricaded? Or would the breakaway air force bomb the palace and stop the crisis that way? My mind went back to that meeting years before at the Malacanang palace. Wasn't there a verse I'd quoted, about…about the palace being…in ruins? My goodness! I suddenly froze with the thought. *Could this really be going to happen?*

I reached for my Bible and quickly found Jeremiah 22, the passage God had used to confirm that I should take FEET to the palace. It was all coming back to me. I recalled the events of that day four years earlier and my warning that a peaceful transition of power would happen only if the Philippine government avoided evil. I was now convinced the Marcos administration had been far from righteous. Many accused friends of the administration of the death of Senator Aquino at Manila International Airport in 1983.

As I came to the end of Jeremiah 22, I stopped and stared at a verse that spoke with a sense of immediacy, as if God was wanting to say something new to me from this chapter. In context, the verse spoke of the wicked king Jehoiachin and what would happen to him. Was God trying to tell me something about President Marcos?

"I will hurl you…into another country…you will never come back to the land you long to return to" (Jer. 22:26–27). I'd worried that the palace would be bombed or that Marcos would fire into the crowds. Even as dictatorial as Marcos was, I still didn't feel he would give such an order. (Later I found out how wrong I was. Only the disobedience of the tank commanders prevented much slaughter and loss of life.)

Was God now telling me that President Marcos would go into exile by way of the words "I will hurl you…into another country…"? That was the question on my mind as I drifted off to sleep.

The next morning I awoke to be greeted with the headlines that Marcos had fled from the Philippines and was on his way to Hawaii!

God had been trying to tell me this would happen. Corazon Aquino was now the undisputed president of the Philippines. With tears in my eyes and a lump in my throat, I later watched the TV images of Mrs. Aquino being sworn in as President of the Republic.

I thought back to what had jumped out of the Bible to me about "going into exile and never seeing his home country again." If the first part has come to pass, I reasoned, so would the second, "You will never come back to the land you long to return to."

The author's training school came to an end, and I returned to Hawaii and to speaking engagements. Publicly I declared that President Marcos would never return to the Philippines. That conviction was severely tested when Margaret and I and our family returned to the Philippines for most of the next year (1987). While we led a YWAM Discipleship Training School on the southern island of Mindanao, Mrs. Aquino was hounded by coup attempts against her administration. Marcos's supporters constantly agitated for the return of their hero. "He is an old man," they wrote in the press. "He should be allowed to return to his home country to die." Even President Aquino said she was considering the possibility.

I didn't share that sentiment. Nor did I feel that that was God's will. There were numerous rumors that Marcos was secretly trying to return to Manila to destabilize the new Aquino government. It was my conviction that there would be civil war if Marcos returned. I felt God lead me to write to President Aquino and cited the scriptures through which God had spoken to me about Marcos.

I don't know whether my letter ever reached her desk. But Mrs. Aquino finally settled on the conviction, shared by the U.S. State Department, that Marcos should not return. Perhaps it was the bloody coup attempt against her government that took eight hundred lives while we were in the Philippines that year that helped change her mind. But that was nothing compared to what would have surely happened in a civil war inspired by Marcos's return.

A year later I flew to the U.S. mainland on a Philippine airliner and sat next to a Filipino lawyer. Falling into conversation with him, I learned he was on his way to Los Angeles to work on Marcos's legal return to the Philippines! I looked around the packed-out plane and marveled at the arrangement. Concluding that God had arranged this "coincidence," I turned to my seatmate and said, "You must not work on this case."

"Why ever not?" he answered in surprise.

I told him what God had revealed to me concerning Marcos's future. I stated without hesitation, "He won't see his homeland again."

I never found out what happened to that lawyer or whether he reported my words to Marcos. But I do know that in 1989 Marcos suddenly became ill and died in Hawaii at the age of seventy-two.

He never saw the Philippines again after going into exile.

Receiving Revelation

As we continue to faithfully intercede over an issue, we can expect God to speak to us. Intercession is hard work, but revelation gives us the encouragement that we're on the right track and that we're to continue to pray. Sometimes God will guide us into a course correction so we pray more according to His will. At other times, God may reveal exactly what evil power to combat.

Years ago, I evangelized beside a New Zealand Maori *pa,* or meetinghouse. Several days later, I began to feel agonizing pain in my back, an unheard-of problem for me. I began to pray and then suddenly found myself rebuking the spirit of a *Tohunga,* or Maori witch doctor. Immediately the pain disappeared and never returned. The apostle Paul says that in spiritual warfare, we are to take "the sword of the Spirit, which is the word of God" (Eph. 6:17). "Word" in that verse is *rhema,* which means a word from God by the Spirit. When I had the acute back pain, naming the evil spirit responsible brought the victory. This is why intercession is likened to war. We have a real enemy, who opposes that which threatens his kingdom.

At the same time, revelation will often lead to action. With the understanding that Marcos was not to return to the Philippines, for example, I was emboldened to write to President Aquino and discourage the lawyer on the airliner. Later, God led me to talk to another highly placed government official.

Another reason for revelation is that it will always increase the level of our fellowship with the Lord. God wishes to commune with us as *friends.* Whereas inanimate objects like the moon and planets obey God by the law of gravity, that doesn't do as much to His heart as people voluntarily fellowshiping and obeying Him. His heart is warmed when we stay in tune with Him.

In response, God then shares Himself, His thoughts, and His plans with His children. This adds to the quality of our walk with God, who never intended our relationship to be devoid of personal encouragement and intimacy.

Jesus said to His disciples, "You are my friends if you obey me. I no longer call you slaves, for a master doesn't confide in his slaves; *now you are my friends,* proved by the fact that I have told you everything the Father told me," (John 15:14–15 TLB, emphasis added). No wonder the apostle Paul wrote, "Devote yourselves to prayer" (Col. 4:2). He knew the intimacy with God that would result if we took that exhortation to heart.

During the dark years of 1939–45, Rees Howell, the director of a Bible college in Wales, felt deeply burdened about the then raging Second World War. As he and his students faithfully interceded four hours each night, God revealed that they were to pray for specific events to come to pass. After four particularly heavy, drawn-out "battles" in prayer, they were encouraged to see God miraculously intervene. They were further heartened by a press article in which a military commentator stated that the Nazi cause was now doomed as a result of four mistakes Hitler had made. These mistakes were the very events, led by God, that Rees Howell and the others had wrestled over.*

God is ready to give us more revelation as we intercede, but it has been my experience that we have to persist in prayer and to *keep to the subject* for this to happen.

---

*See chapters 35 and 36 of *Rees Howell Intercessor* by Norman Grubb (Lutterworth Press, 1973).

fifteen

Giving Up Rights

To increase the prospect of victory during World War II, the citizens of the warring nations often endured hardships. A young man's duty in those dark days was to join the armed service and risk serious injury and death. Back home, men and women put in long hours of backbreaking work by day and were subject to blackouts and bombing raids at night. Commodities such as gasoline, meat, sugar, and flour were rationed and even completely denied.

As Christians, we're right now in a war of even greater importance, with grimmer potential consequences—a war between heaven and hell. It is the age-long struggle between the forces of good and evil. To increase our effectiveness against the powers of darkness, God may at times ask us to surrender our right to something precious: to our money, to be close to our families, to our reputation, or even to marriage. The biggest right He might ask us to give up is our right to life itself.

I genuinely thought I was prepared to die for Christ, but an event one day suddenly made me realize how conditional my readiness was.

*I*n an earlier book, I recorded the tragic deaths of Mike and Janice Shelling, two of our friends in the Philippines. Mike had worked with Margaret and me for seven years and had been a vital part of our ministry. When Janice later joined our staff, we'd encouraged their friendship and so had taken a parental interest in their lives together. It was more than their deaths that shocked us, however. It was the way they had died—stabbed in their home on a street where our own family had once lived. We wept for days at their passing before I flew from Hawaii to Baguio to attend the funeral. As I walked the streets after dark, I experienced an unexpected depth of fear I'd never known before.

With the passage of time, I convinced myself that the Shellings' deaths were unique. To my knowledge, no other Baguio missionary had been murdered. Since Mike and Janice's home had been ransacked and valuables taken, presumably the motive for the murders was robbery.

The following year, I felt God put it on my heart to organize a missions school at the University of the Nations campus in Kona, Hawaii, that would start in January 1987. After the classroom phase of the school, we planned to take students to Davao City in the south of the Philippines. We'd all work with Graeme and Mary Jones, our dear friends from Baguio days who had pioneered YWAM Davao.

Davao City, the third-largest population center in the country, had long held a special place in my heart. I had helped Dal Walker during one of his tent campaigns in Davao, and after Margaret and I were married, our first home in the

Philippines was in this city. But during the 1980s, the military arm of the communist movement terrorized the area while on other parts of the island, Muslim separatists fought the government. Thankfully, I'd heard that hostilities from both factions had calmed down. Excitedly I began recruiting students for the missions school.

Before the school started, Margaret and I visited friends and family in New Zealand for two months. We were packing for our flight back to Hawaii when Margaret was called to the phone upstairs. After hanging up, she walked slowly down the stairs.

"That was the YWAM office," she said in a subdued tone. "One of the female YWAM staff members in Davao City, Randy Adams, has just been stabbed to death. Black-shirted men forced their way into the house in broad daylight, killing her and her Filipina worker. No valuables were taken."

A chill stabbed my heart as I stopped packing. Who were these black-shirted people? Were they communists or Muslim rebels? We didn't know Randy or her worker, but it didn't matter. We were deeply shocked at the incident. We talked for a while, struggling with a myriad of thoughts.

Quietly we resumed placing clothes in our bags for the flight. Our spirits were still subdued as we boarded the Continental Airlines jet headed for Hawaii. The lightly booked flight allowed us plenty of room for sleeping on the overnight journey. But the five seats I stretched out on didn't help. I couldn't sleep.

Repeatedly, my mind recalled the shocking murders. Whereas I reasoned the Shelling deaths were occasioned by robbery, I couldn't attribute theft to this case, since no valuables were taken. What, then, was the motive? What did the black shirts mean? Was this a conspiracy against missionaries?

Against YWAM? What did this mean for our future? I had no answers.

Over and over, my questions and worries surged like giant waves through my mind as we jetted through the night. How safe was it to take Margaret and our three boys to Davao? And a team? Still ringing in my ears was an emphatic statement from Margaret's uncle the day we left New Zealand.

"I wouldn't take my wife to that part of the world."

And he hadn't even heard of the latest killing!

I continued to worry over the next couple of months, both in Hawaii and on a trip to California to visit those who had applied to our school. In the back of my mind, my greatest fear was not losing my life. *It was being stabbed to death.*

The idea of being shot in the back when I wasn't aware of danger did not bother me. The Scriptures tell us that to be absent from the body is to be present with the Lord (2 Cor. 5:8). But the thought of being stabbed to death terrified me, so much so that when I buckled up to drive from Los Angeles to northern California, I prayed testily, "Lord, I'd rather die in this car today than die like Randy and her helper!"

As I traveled, I felt obligated to share with the prospective students that they would not be free from danger. I mentioned in passing that YWAMers had lost their lives in the Philippines in recent years.

I stayed in the homes of my prospective students and fielded many questions. One father asked me point-blank, "Can you guarantee that our son will not die if he takes this trip with you?"

"No, I'm sorry I can't guarantee that," I quietly conceded.

"Why can't you?" he exploded. "It's not right that my son could lose his life!"

It was ironic. I had my own fears to contend with. In response, I told him of my younger sister Julia, a missionary who had traveled the world. Yet while on a New Zealand road in the middle of the night she was killed when her driver fell asleep at the wheel returning from an Easter Christian convention.

"You know," I continued, "no place is really safe."

Back in Hawaii I continued to wrestle with my thoughts. On campus once a quarter, YWAM holds a day of prayer and fasting to which all staff and students are invited. On that November day of 1986, I still worried about taking our family to Davao. I sat in the open pavilion praying with the others just as I had on a previous fasting day when God had originally given me the idea of taking the outreach to that city. Suddenly I sensed His gentle voice say to my inner man, *Don't you think My grace would be sufficient at such a time as being stabbed to death?* I immediately saw my unbelief. Of course! God wouldn't ask of me more than I could handle. He'd be there with me. That's His character!

"O Lord, You're right!" I prayed contritely. "Your grace would be sufficient. I accept that now. Thank You!"

Postscript

Twenty-one of us left for the Philippines after the lecture phase of the school ended in March 1987. Most of us remained in Davao far beyond the length of the official three-month outreach. Margaret and I and some of the Kona team stayed on to lead the six-month Discipleship Training School (DTS) mentioned in the previous chapter. The fruitfulness of our ministry was beyond expectations, and in the atmosphere of a loving DTS student body, our family thrived. Even now, that experience stands out as one of the highlights of our lives.

But there were dangers. A house across the road was shot at one night. A couple of our students were held up at knifepoint and relieved of valuables. On the DTS outreach, a team of volunteers went to the predominately Muslim province of Sulu known for kidnapping foreigners. Before I visited the team, God quickened to me a passage from 2 Chronicles 15:5–7 that I'd come to no harm.

I could be very thankful for that word. Ten days before the team sailed into the area, a bomb exploded at the Catholic church, killing four. Just two days before the team arrived, another bomb exploded in the building next to the Protestant church where they were to stay. It was rumored that the Protestant church would be the next target. When I arrived for my visit, we sat around the table at that church at night knowing we could all die that evening. God's grace was mightily present, and I felt no fear.

Although I heard much later that I had been targeted to be kidnapped, God diverted me from their noose when I suddenly felt impressed to leave at midday the next day on a ship for a neighboring group of islands. I learned later that after I left, a mysterious jeep carrying unknown men waited for two hours just outside where I'd been staying.

Giving Up Rights

Giuseppe Garibaldi, the man largely responsible for the unification of modern Italy, once attracted recruits to his cause by declaring that he offered them hardship, hunger, thirst, rags, sleepless nights, foot sores in the long marches, innumerable privations, and *victory*. Far from being repelled by his challenge, young Italians followed him.

Why, then, should Jesus demand less than earthly leaders? He doesn't, for He declared, "If anyone comes to me and does not hate his father and mother, his wife and children, his brothers and sisters—yes, even his own life—*he cannot be my disciple.* And anyone who does not carry his cross and follow me cannot be my disciple" (Luke 14:26–27, emphasis added). To follow Jesus will therefore involve giving up certain rights that may include the following.

1. *Our reputation.* A man of God once told me, "There has never been someone greatly used of God who did not lose his reputation (through no fault of his own) at some stage." It is not hard to follow his reasoning, for Abraham, Moses, Daniel, and the early apostles all lost their reputations as they obeyed God. So did Joseph and Mary, the earthly guardians of Jesus, for many thought they had sinned. Even thirty years later, the legitimacy of Jesus' birth was still sneered at (John 8:41, 48). This is part of the cost of being used of God. Jesus actually went further than all of us and *made himself of no reputation* (Phil. 2:7 KJV).

2. *Our family.* When Jesus talked about "hating father and mother" (Luke 14:26), He employed a Hebrew way of teaching by using a contrast to make a comparison. Obviously, that phrase has to be taken in the light of Matthew 10:37–38, "Anyone who loves his father or mother more than me is not worthy of me...." Our love for Christ is to be supreme, even above the natural affection for our parents. Jesus had to make the terms of discipleship clear, for He was aware that those who followed Him could be rejected by their families (Matt. 10:36).

3. *Marriage.* The apostle Paul did not prohibit marriage, but he did see the value of giving up this right (1 Cor. 7:8). It would have been difficult for him to have accomplished what he did as a married man. Jesus even spoke of those who "renounced marriage because of the kingdom of heaven" (Matt. 19:12).

One day years ago, I preached, "It is usually God's will for everyone to marry." A woman in the audience later drew me aside and politely said, "You should not have said that.

Christian young women today far outnumber Christian young men. Mathematically it is impossible for every Christian woman to marry." I immediately saw her point. Short of a revival of monumental proportions, she was right.

4. *Life itself.* We in the West are very protective of human life, and so we should be. But perhaps we are too protective. To reach certain areas of the world, Christians must be willing to lay down their lives for Christ. In the early days of this modern missionary era, English missionaries knew they would die of disease in West Africa just three months after arrival. That didn't stop them. They simply took coffins with them in which they were buried three months later!

When Jesus said that unless we take up our cross and follow Him, we cannot be His disciples, His listeners understood that anyone carrying his cross was on his way to be crucified. Jesus meant that *all* believers—not just holy men of God—need to be willing to die for His cause. To lay down our lives for Christ, then, is not weird, but a noble act.

We know that God is a gracious God. There is nothing we give up that He doesn't lavishly compensate. Jesus gave up the privilege of marriage, family, reputation, and His own life. Afterward, God exalted Him to the highest place (Phil. 2:9). While that station belongs to Jesus and Him alone, it does illustrate a principle.

5. *Etcetera.* In the service of God, we are often called on to sacrifice our time, our money, our positions—even our food, at times, as God leads us into prayer and fasting (Matt. 6:16–18; 9:15). For those who are married but must travel, it means giving up many comforts, including intimacy with their spouse. For parents who have children called to be missionaries, it means giving up the privilege of seeing them and their grandchildren on a regular basis. I think of the sacrifice my own parents were called to and thank them for it.

God cannot force us to love Him, but He can woo us. He has done that through the Cross and by a variety of tangible ways. In response, we lovingly obey Him and even think up ways to serve Him more effectively. Christians once sold themselves into slavery, for example, to gain access to a Caribbean island to witness for Christ. In more recent years, missionaries have surrendered their passports and taken up foreign citizenship to legally stay where they were called. The apostle Paul wrote, "Though I am free and belong to no man, I make myself a *slave* to everyone, to win as many as possible" (1 Cor. 9:19, emphasis added). The reason? So that "this gospel of the kingdom will be preached in the whole world as a testimony to all nations, and then the end will come" (Matt 24:14). Then we will be forever with the Lord (1 Thess. 4:17)!

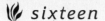 *sixteen*

Valuing Praise and Worship

At times of great victory and during seasons of God's nearness, I love to worship God. But I must confess that at other times over the years, praising God was often a formality. I knew I should start my prayer times with unhurried worship, but often I'd go straight to my requests. I now deeply regret that lifestyle. Because salvation is loving and knowing God, we should seek unhurried fellowship with the Lord.

Worship is a heart response of adoration and love for God and His promises. Worship should be the foundation of all aspects of the Christian life, though at its deepest level, it is a response to God Himself. It often paves the way for the extraordinary and the miraculous.

In 1989 I led a school outreach to India, where our team helped an evangelistic campaign night after night in a dimly lit field. After the meeting one night, the Kona, Hawaii, students and I were standing near the wooden platform, when suddenly my name was called.

Wheeling around, I looked into the worried face of the young Indian campaign coordinator. With him stood a sari-clad woman. As I stole a glance at the fear-filled young Indian beside him, he shared his concern.

"Just four days ago," he began in urgent tones, "someone placed a Hindu curse on her tongue. She has not been able to speak since. Her name is Lila. Could you please pray for her deliverance?"

I swallowed hard. It was late. It had also been a long, humid day, with the temperature up around 105°F. Even now, that warm, moist air wrapped itself around me like a blanket. More to the point, I didn't feel that I had the faith for a situation this big. Everything within me felt like saying, "No. Please have someone else pray for her." But I was embarrassed to say no. Evangelist D. G. S. Dhinakaran and the other spiritual "heavies" had already left. Because I'd taught hundreds of counselors for the campaign, I felt obligated to at least have a go. I was glad, however, that most of the crowd of sixty thousand had already left the field.

During the final weeks of our lecture phase in Kona, the students and I had been instructed in how to deal with this type of request. Encouragingly, the Kona instructor had been a convert from YWAM Baguio who had become a pastor. I was about to learn just how much of that lesson had been absorbed.

Calling the students together, I explained Lila's situation. To my amazement, the students responded enthusiastically to the challenge. While I didn't feel great faith myself, I felt proud of them. Encouraged by their excitement, I led in prayer, and the students enthusiastically followed one by one.

Ten minutes later, Lila's condition was no different, and frankly I wasn't surprised. But we didn't give up. During the week of instruction in Kona, the visiting Filipino pastor had encouraged us. "Miracles are more likely to happen if you keep on praying." Suddenly one of my more vocal and enthusiastic students had an inspiration.

"I think she has a fetish around her neck," she whispered hoarsely somewhere near my ear. I looked more closely at Lila in the poor light. For the first time I noticed a band of beads around her neck, and I knew what I'd have to do. I invited her to discard the fetish and renounce the deity it represented. She looked at me intently and then wagged her head side to side in the distinctive Indian way of saying yes. Deliberately she removed the fetish. To really make sure she understood our position, I asked her to forsake the deity by following me in prayer by wagging her head in agreement. She complied.

Once again we resumed our prayer for her, except this time I exhorted the team to worship the Lord, which they did with great enthusiasm. Again I was proud of this dedicated group.

Five minutes later, something happened. Lila spoke! In fact, she fluently thanked Jesus with us. We were ecstatic! We burst into spontaneous joy and worshiped the Lord, hardly believing the impossible had happened. Whereas earlier we had praised the Lord "in obedience," we were now praising the Lord in rapturous, wholehearted joy! An hour later, Lila was still saying, "Thank You, Jesus, thank You, Jesus!" as if her whole life depended on it.

Thrilled with her healing, she returned to the nightly meetings, each time bringing a neighbor or a friend with her. The miracle had shown God's character to her, and she wanted to share that with others. To us, God had demonstrated the value of worship as an act of our faith in His almighty power!

Back in India nearly a decade later, I recalled God's miracle with Lila, especially when another incident occurred that reinforced my understanding of the power that praise can release for God's glory. In a missions school, I shared how God had, as a result of prayer, granted King Hezekiah an extension of fifteen years to his life. As I looked out over the students in the classroom, I felt the Lord tell me to stop my teaching and ask the students to pair off. They were to pray over each other's requests, knowing that a compassionate God was listening. I hesitated for a moment and then made the announcement.

Later, as the praying finished, I reminded the students that we were to praise and worship God as an act of faith that God had truly heard our prayers. "Let's worship the Lord," I exhorted. About ten minutes later, the class came alive as we sang, "O come, let us adore Him." The atmosphere was suddenly charged with love and reverence for God.

I was about to stand and resume my teaching when the school leader, a young Indian man in his twenties, intervened. He exhorted the class to continue to worship God by assuming the position most worshipful to them. Many continued to sit, some knelt, others stood while a few even lay prostrate before the Lord.

For the next hour God poured out His Spirit. Sensing the leading of the Lord, I prayed over several of the students. Later a young Indian staff girl told me she'd been weeping in discouragement earlier that morning, wanting to resign from her present role. Radiantly she now told me that when I laid hands on her in prayer, she felt God's power pulsate through her body! A young man testified to a similar experience. Yet another young woman, just six months in the faith, told me it was the first time she had ever felt God's presence! It was a supernatural time from the Lord for many of them!

Obviously there were several factors at work in that classroom, but a very significant one was the unhurried time of worship. God responds when we demonstrate we believe Him through our worship and praise!

Valuing Praise and Worship

Psalm 100:2 reads, "Serve the LORD with gladness: come before his presence with singing" (KJV). One day while memorizing that verse, it suddenly struck me: Singing to someone, like a mother to her newborn baby or a young man to his date, is a sign of love. In a similar way, we as Christians are to come before the Lord with love in our hearts.

That thought made immediate sense, for salvation is loving and knowing God (John 17:3; Luke 7:47; 10:25–28). Worship is a prime expression of that love. It takes away the sense that we must cajole and beg God into hearing us. It also corrects the human tendency to immediately present our "shopping lists" at the beginning of our prayer times!

Later in Psalm 100 I memorized, "Enter his gates with thanksgiving and his courts with praise…" (verse 4). The gates here refer to the entrance to the temple in Jerusalem, whereas the courts represent the holy place. Being thankful for what God has done is a good way to start our quiet times with God. But we should move on from there to a higher form of thankfulness, which is to praise Him for who He is and for His flawless character. This is true worship.

We are to worship God whether He has done something spectacular lately or not. Whether we live in peace or war. Whether He has answered our latest prayer or not. Because His character is always the same, always benevolent and always unselfish, we can praise and worship Him at all times and in all situations. He is the uncreated, magnificent Creator.

Worshiping God *before* He answers our prayer is an important Christian experience, for it tells God that our faith is active.

We are not just sitting back and watching. We are believing He will do something. I am continually challenged by Paul and Silas when they worshiped God in a smelly, damp, unhygienic prison cell despite the agony of the flogging they had just endured. Their example is clear. Despite our circumstances, we are to constantly praise God for who He is. But again, notice what happened *after* they had worshiped. There was an earthquake, which eventually led to the conversion of the pagan jailer and his entire family (Acts 16:23–34).

Another result from worshiping God is that we hear His voice in guidance. God gave the early apostles clear guidance after a time of worshiping the Lord and fasting. Notice it was "worshiping the Lord and fasting" not "fasting and prayer" in this particular incidence (Acts 13:1–3).

Consider the amount of time Anna the prophetess spent in worship before the Lord. "She never left the temple but worshiped night and day, fasting and praying" (Luke 2:37). When Joseph and Mary brought the infant Jesus to the temple, God gave Anna insight as to who this baby really was—the coming Redeemer!

Worshiping God brings so many things into balance. When we worship God in spirit and in truth, our hearts are exposed to God's light. It is therefore impossible to carry a grudge, disobey God, or dwell on a lustful thought. It's also hard to be depressed when we feel His presence in worship.

From the story of King Jehoshaphat, who sent worshipers into battle against Ammon and Moab ahead of his fighting men (2 Chron. 20:14–23), we learn a vital lesson: Worship is an essential ingredient in spiritual warfare, just as it was God-ordained in Old Testament battles. In both physical warfare and its spiritual counterpart, the battle can be long and hard. Worshiping the Lord not only lightens the load, but also reminds us who brings the victory. While we are to rebuke the devil as we pray, worship reminds us that victory ultimately comes from God.

Like so many other things about worship, it puts a great God right at the center of everything—where He really belongs!

seventeen

Continuing On in Discipleship

The second law of thermodynamics tells us that physical items left to themselves will deteriorate. Order turns to chaos. Iron rusts, wood rots, and weeds grow. What is true in the physical realm is true in the spiritual. If we are not walking with God, our spiritual and moral lives will slowly decline. Church history is a sad illustration of this truth. No wonder Jesus appeared to the early Church before the end of the first century to ask them to return to their first love (Rev. 2:4–5).

A disciple must continue to press into God rather than drift or live on past victories. How easy it is to just coast spiritually. How simple it is to let the muscles of discipleship atrophy or grow weak. In late 1998, I was brought painfully face-to-face with this grim truth.

In 1998 Margaret and I spent four months in the Philippines helping to lead a School of Evangelism. As the time to return to Hawaii approached, God laid it on my heart that I was to leave on December 23, a week after Margaret and the boys. However, when I tried to make the booking, China Airlines told me I would be number nineteen on the waiting list! As the young woman peered into her computer screen, she said, "But I can book you all the way to Hawaii on the day before, the twenty-second."

Immediately I faced a dilemma. Should I take that secure booking? Or should I place my name on the waiting list for the twenty-third? What if I was unsuccessful in getting a seat? I could be stuck in Manila while my family celebrated Christmas Day in Hawaii without me. *Why not go with the guaranteed seat?* Despite my misgivings about disobeying what I felt God had said, I told the agent, "Please book me on the twenty-second."

Pushing back the glass doors of the China Airlines office a few minutes later, I felt guilty. I tried justifying my actions. Wasn't my family in Hawaii important, too? Was it right for me to be away from them on Christmas Day? Even as I tried to console myself with this excuse, I felt appalled at my shameful unbelief. *Faith really is like a muscle,* I mused as I walked along M. Adriatico Street and then waited to cross a few blocks down the road. *And because I haven't been exercising mine for a while, it has weakened.*

Over lunch with a friend at a fast-food restaurant on United Nations Avenue, I could hardly concentrate on our conversation. All I could think about were the words whirling around inside my head: *God told you to leave the twenty-third, but you've booked for the twenty-second!* The impression was not harsh, but matter-of-fact.

By the end of the meal, I determined to do what the Lord had originally said. I would trust God and leave the consequences to Him. I walked back to M. Adriatico Street, swung open the glass doors of China Airlines, and asked the same ticket clerk to change my booking. I was now on the waiting list for the twenty-third.

Later that afternoon when I visited the office of OMF Literature, the Philippine agents for my books *We Cannot But Tell* and *Adventures in Naked Faith,* I was in for a surprise. Channel 7 in Manila wanted to interview me about my books, now selling in both Christian and secular bookstores. They would schedule me on their breakfast show in the next few days. The date the TV station finally came up with was December 22, the day I had planned to leave the country. No wonder God had said the day of departure was to be the twenty-third!

The day before the TV show, I had plenty of time to seek God as I zipped along the highway on a six-hour bus ride. In one of my prayer times for the interview, I felt impressed that I was to share the gospel more than promote my books. My heart leapt. *Of course! Most of the viewers will not be believers anyway.* I readily accepted the challenge. On the set the next day I recounted the story of the lost bag (chapter 11) and how my companion had been changed from his lifestyle of doing drugs. That was one of the reasons Jesus came two thousand years ago—to change us. I mentioned I'd formerly been a shoplifter and that Christ had transformed me. Jesus had changed a friend with a violent temper and others who had attempted suicide or had slept around. That is why the gospel is the Good News. We *can* be changed! "If anyone is in Christ," I declared, "he is a new creation. The old has gone and the new has come."

The show went out live and nationwide, and I was sobered by the fact that this opportunity to speak to a nation could have been so easily missed.

Continuing On in Discipleship

A disciple never arrives on this earth; he or she is always a learner. Even by our mistakes (as in the story just told), we must continue to learn. In essence, discipleship requires getting to know, love, and worship the God of the universe; learning to hear His voice; and stepping out in faith to do His bidding. His will for our lives is always to be part of the *cause* by which the gospel goes into all the earth.

Learning means that we press into God for even greater revelation as to His character. It is when we understand the nature and character of God that we find His instructions easier to obey and our walk with Him more rewarding. A trust in God's character says, "I know You are a just and wonderful God. Therefore what You say must be the best for all concerned." I cannot overemphasize the importance of making a continuing study of God's character a vital part of your life.

I did get on the China Airlines flight December 23 to enjoy Christmas with family and friends, but God would have been just and good even if I hadn't. His character is perfect no matter what happens. I know He is actively willing the highest good for everyone (including you and me) all the time. That is what love is!

In a real sense, it is not how we *start* our walk with the Lord that is of the greatest consequence to God, but how we *finish*. We have already seen how Eli the priest and King Saul messed up on God's will for their lives (chapter 8). As wonderful as their potential for God was, they regrettably were not finishers. It is

God's will for you and me to finish our course, just as the apostle Paul finished his. In 2 Timothy 4:7, Paul wrote, "I have fought the good fight, I have finished the race, I have kept the faith."

How, then, do we keep ourselves continuing on in discipleship and on the cutting edge for God? Here are some suggestions.

1. *By reading the Word of God.* One purpose of the Word of God is for us to get to know the *God* of the Word (Deut. 17:19). As the knowledge of His character and the knowledge of His ways touch our hearts, faith increases, and we feel like doing His "exploits" (Dan. 11:32 KJV).

Many times something warms my heart as I read a certain verse or concept in the Bible. It may be new light on an old thought, the exact answer I need for a certain problem, or the very thing I should pray concerning a friend or nation. It could be correction or even guidance. I keep a spiritual journal and often write down my thoughts and the Scripture that brought them to mind. It can be spiritually invigorating to go back and read those thoughts at a later date.

The Bible tells us that all Scripture is profitable "for teaching, rebuking, correcting and training in righteousness, so that the man of God may be thoroughly equipped for every good work." (2 Tim. 3:16–17). There is no way we can be an effective disciple of Christ without loving His Word. Job said, "I have esteemed the words of his mouth more than my necessary food" (Job 23:12 KJV).

2. *By memorizing Scripture.* To be frank, sometimes when I start my day, I don't *feel* like reading my Bible. But if I memorize a line or two of Scripture, it leads me right into a meaningful time with the Lord and His Word. As I memorize, the truth of the Word of God begins to mingle with my spirit. That in turn energizes me as I am encouraged, challenged, and corrected. The more I respond to the Lord, the more He "restores my soul."

3. By fasting and praying. Do you ever feel spiritually dry? The best way I have found to quicken my spiritual life is to fast and pray, even if it is for just a few meals. I seem to focus in on the Lord, His will, and His Word much better as a result.

John Wesley and the early Methodists fasted until 3 P.M. twice a week. It has been suggested that they simply followed the example the early apostles set once Jesus returned to heaven. Recently, as I read the journal of someone on the front lines of evangelism in a pagan country, I was touched that he and his wife reserved a day each week to fast and pray. It helped me understand why their lives burned so brightly in that dark land—and why they were so effective for Christ.

We know that the apostle Paul's missionary journeys started as a result of guidance received during a time of praying and fasting (Acts 13:1–3). I have found that guidance comes more clearly during or after a time of prayer and fasting.* A word of caution: It is always wise to consult your physician before embarking on a fast of any length.

4. By deliberately looking for opportunities to witness. Jesus said He came to serve mankind and give Himself as a ransom for many. He obviously wants us to continue to spread His valuable message throughout the earth. Therefore, it is godly for us to be thinking of ways to further His cause.

If you are new to evangelism, don't start by approaching the fiercest-looking gangster that you can find! Pray about sharing the gospel with someone you know. Consider asking the person to accompany you to see a Christian movie or attend a Christian concert or church service. The more you witness, the more natural you will become as you share your life in Christ with others.

---

*An excellent book on the subject of fasting is *The Coming Revival* by Bill Bright (New Life Publications, 1995).

We are, of course, to witness for God's sake. We must see the unsaved as He sees them—as people He loves—rather than as people useful to our "cause." An interesting by-product is the development in our own lives. Usually when I witness, I am drawn closer to the Lord, His Word, and the people He died for. I also feel more grateful for my salvation. If I've witnessed to someone with horrific problems, I say to myself, "Wow! I don't have anything to complain about!" Witnessing gives us a more objective and healthier look at things.

5. *By having fellowship with those of like mind.* We all know that a coal from a fire goes out much quicker if set apart by itself, or that a sheep separated from the others bunched up on a bitter windswept slope won't survive. It is amazing to me how often Christians don't seek out other Christians of like mind. Endeavor to meet with those who want to pray, obey God, and believe Him for the impossible. God never intended for us to be an island. We are to be encouraged by those who want to be effective disciples of Jesus. Ask God to link you in love with those of like mind.

6. *By keeping informed.* If you know what career or ministry (or geographical area of the world) you are called to, you can start reading biographies and other relevant books now. You can also contact those who have a similar calling on their lives, asking for their input and advice—especially those who have been following their calling for many years.

As you do this, God may confirm His will to you. Or it may become apparent that God has something else in store. Either way, the exercise will prove useful. But keep in mind that as important as accumulating knowledge might be, it is not an end in itself. Academic knowledge alone will not get the job of discipleship done. The experiential knowledge of God and His ways is the greatest need in our lives, for the more we hear from God, the more effective we will be.

Conclusion

As you travel the path of discipleship, don't forget to consider that while Jesus *called* the Twelve during the early part of his earthly ministry (Luke 6:12–16), He didn't *commission* them until he spent years shaping and training them (Matt. 28:16–20). We should be encouraged by how like us the Twelve were. They often lacked faith, they argued over who was to be the greatest, they fell asleep when they should have prayed, and they had difficulty casting out a demon. We have to take to heart that Jesus did not abandon them. He continued to shape their lives and *believe* in them. God doesn't give up on us easily.

Discipleship—the process of learning to follow Jesus—is vital to our work for God's kingdom. As we learn more of His ways, we become an increasingly effective tool in the hands of the Holy Spirit. Remember that between the two experiences of calling and commissioning, the disciples were used of God, even as Jesus continued to chisel His image in them.

From my first bumbling steps as a disciple, God has been patient with me. I am still a disciple because I am still a learner. He will be with you, too, as you steadfastly set your hand to the plow and never look back. Whatever you do, keep praying. *Devote* yourself to prayer. Every disciple is both a worshiper and an intercessor.

May the Lord continue to develop in us a more Christlike character, the ability to hear His voice better, and the desire to love Him more deeply and follow Him more closely.

Happy discipleship!

❦ ministry update

We are still on staff of the University of the Nations in Kona, Hawaii. Margaret has been the university librarian for several years but also teaches the Word of God and uses her considerable musical skills. I teach, travel, write, and coordinate intercession efforts on campus. Since 1987, I have led seven YWAM mission schools and taken those students to Asia.

Our four months in Baguio City last year brought back a flood of memories as we fellowshiped with Filipinos from the student center years of 1973–83. Some who attended those meetings years ago are now pastoring or in missionary work or holding responsible positions either in the Philippines or abroad.

It was fun for me to do some of the very things I enjoyed in the seventies. One week during the lecture phase of our School of Evangelism, I took the students from class to class preaching the gospel in one of the colleges. They were powerful days. I also preached and witnessed in Burnham Park with our students and spoke in churches. Instead of being interviewed on radio this time, I was interviewed several times on local cable TV (in addition to the broadcast from Manila mentioned in the last chapter).

Our two youngest boys, Warren and Hudson, came with us and were thoroughly spoiled by the hospitality of our Baguio students. Our two older boys, Mark and Stuart, live in New Zealand. Mark is now a civil engineer, and Stuart works as a computer programmer. Both are doing exceptionally well in their vocations.

And our future? We are not completely sure. But we know that it will have something to do with "this gospel of the kingdom" being preached in all the world.